P9-BZF-684

How to Make People Want to Work Harder and Smarter—
Advice from the Nation's Foremost Authority on
Performance Improvement:

*It is time to put the current crisis in leadership behind us,
by capitalizing on the universal desires of men and women
to serve themselves and humankind in purposeful activities
and relationships.*

*Ambitious, perceptive managers can learn to motivate em-
ployees to the kind of excellence that comes from personal
commitment. This book tells how. . . .*

THE
PSYCHOLOGY
OF
LEADERSHIP

"A clear and systematic view of the psychological underpin-
nings of good management . . . Offers insight and assistance
for anyone seriously interested in improving his or her management style."

—Robert M. Price,
President, Control Data Corporation

DR. JARD DEVILLE is an internationally known mo-
tivational psychologist whose diverse career includes
leadership service in academic, clinical and business
areas. Among his previous books are *Nice Guys Finish
First, Lovers for Life* and, in Japanese, *Leadership
Power.*

From the MENTOR Executive Library

THE PSYCHOLOGY OF LEADERSHIP

MANAGING RESOURCES AND RELATIONSHIPS

DR. JARD DeVILLE

A MENTOR BOOK

NEW AMERICAN LIBRARY

NEW YORK AND SCARBOROUGH, ONTARIO

Copyright © 1984 by Jard DeVille

This is an authorized reprint of a hardcover edition published by
Farnsworth Publishing Company, Inc.

Library of Congress Catalog Card Number: 84-62173

SIGNET, SIGNET CLASSIC, MENTOR, PLUME, MERIDIAN AND NAL BOOKS
are published *in the United States* by New American Library,
1633 Broadway, New York, New York 10019,
in Canada by The New American Library of Canada Limited,
81 Mack Avenue, Scarborough, Ontario M1L 1M8

First Mentor Printing, May, 1985

1 2 3 4 5 6 7 8 9

PRINTED IN THE UNITED STATES OF AMERICA

To the memory of Ian Forrester, who drew together the Australian blokes who were insistent that this should be published as they participated in the "Capitalizing On Human Motivation Seminar."

Acknowledgments

No one has contributed more to this book than has Joseph Hraboski. As the Director of Executive Programs at the University of Arizona, he drew into the Executive Development Conference many people who offered concepts, confirmation, and comradeship through the years. Edwin Flippo, Jay Galbreath, James LaSalle, Dave Nott, Gordon Zimmerman *et al*. We didn't always agree, but it was never dull!

For The Reader

I recently heard what could well be the death rattle of a great civilization. I heard it in the loud voices of two factory managers who were at the end of their patience. In Sydney, Australia, an angry executive shouted that the only way to restore productivity would be to line his striking employees against a wall and shoot every third one.

His American counterpart in Los Angeles was less bloody-minded but no less frustrated by his failure to win the commitment of his workers. He advocated a major economic depression to return them to their senses so they would never again challenge his power. His business would suffer and his earnings decline, he admitted, but he felt it would be worth it to get the labor issue settled once and for all. He may have had his wish granted, since his company is now working at half capacity and he is struggling to survive.

I took neither man seriously, since they were both half out of their minds with frustration and were attacking in anger, but as they blustered, it became painfully obvious that neither had any idea of what is happening in our civilization. And neither had a viable plan for ending the crippling adversary relationship that made conflict inevitable. Too few men and women in management have captured a vision of what a community of achievers could become. The large majority is trapped in an antiquated philosophy of leadership that relies upon interpersonal power; when that fails, they are vulnerable to our Asian and European competition.

We have, in the English-speaking world, suffered the massive leadership failure documented in *Harvard Business Review*. We have spent decades in ignorance, selfishness, and neglect. Our leadership failure has included a major loss of vision. There has also been an unwillingness to learn from the social and behavioral scientists, unlike the Japanese who have done it so well. Most damaging of all, however, has been our failure to build satisfying communities of achievers that utilize the dynamic, creative human spirit that produced our civilization in the first place.

It is time to put that failure behind us, to harness the human element by embracing it and capitalizing on the universal desire of men and women to serve themselves and humankind in purposeful activities and relationships. Fortunately, I am finding signs that more perceptive Western managers are beginning to understand how productivity and quality can be restored in our organizations.

I recently spoke about the need to harness motivation and creativity with the executives in my seminar at the University of Arizona. I acknowledged the need for better government cooperation, for improved technology, for lower interest rates, and for freedom from the tyranny of the quarterly report. I then insisted that a new philosophy of leadership is needed to better utilize the great reservoir of human ability that exists in every organization. In the Executive Development Conference, I told the two dozen fast-track executives from Saudi Arabia, France, Latin America, Australia, and the United States that we must turn our organizations into surrogate communities in which people invest their lives at tasks or in relationships that are important to them personally. I concluded by saying that in no other way could an executive or manager further a career more effectively. It was significant that every man and woman in the conference agreed with my summation of the present reality for our organizations.

There is a point to this, and I cannot help but recall it every time I hear managers and supervisors talking about the disloyalty and lack of commitment of their employees: *Every man-*

agement team receives the level of performance from the employees that the team consistently reinforces.

Unfortunately, in our English-speaking nations, the level of performance is frequently *not* what the leaders wanted or expected.

This book is about becoming a more successful manager by harnessing what we now know about quality and productivity. The research is in—any group that becomes what I call a community of achievers can maintain its level of productivity with a 33% reduction in labor costs, with a 25% reduction in floor space, and with a 66% reduction in inventory. Any manager who cannot build a career on those figures probably has no business cluttering the territory!

Jard DeVille, Ph.D.
Sydney, Australia, 1983

Contents

PART THREE

Style And Substance

PART ONE

PATTERNS
THAT
AFFECT
PERFORMANCE

1

New Era—Greater Challenges

Leon Trotsky is not widely respected by large numbers of business men and women, but he made several statements that bring into focus some of the major challenges faced by managers in an era of constant turmoil. During the confusion of the Russian Revolution, the Old Bolshevik said that anyone who wanted only to be left alone in peace to do his work had chosen a terrible century in which to be born. He concluded that trying to reorganize a society was like trying to revitalize a cemetery. Trotsky was correct on both counts, for deep within all kinds of organizations is the desire to keep things as they were when the members first learned them.

Many people live with the illusion that humans enjoy change. The fact is, however, that we seldom want important things to change unless the benefits

3

are immediate and significant. Even when there is an obvious advantage to changing, many people have difficulty adjusting to new circumstances and relationships. For example, the entertainment industry has produced many actors and singers who were unable to successfully handle sudden fame and wealth. In many business and professional organizations, rapid change can have similar disruptive results when people are forced, frequently against their will, to adapt to resources and relationships they resent. They resist for so long that the organizations become crippled.

Managers and professionals like dentists, attorneys, and physicians, who are responsible for leading their employees to achieve together, are frequently the causes of many problems in their own organizations. They yearn, frequently unconsciously, to continue working through the concepts and skills they learned in the beginning. They do so because changes in relationships, techniques, and responsibilities force us to rethink ideas we already mastered, and to adapt when it seems obvious that we usually want others to do the adapting in our organizations.

For example, several years ago, when the demise of large automobile engines became obvious, one young manager was called to a meeting where he was told that his test group would be evaluating the reliability of the Chrysler Corporation's new power plant for domestic sales. When he asked about the engine, he found it to be a massive thing that produced more than 300 horsepower with a commensurate fuel consumption. He protested that the competition was adjusting to rising fuel costs by developing fuel-efficient engines and that Chrysler should be doing the same thing.

His manager immediately pinned him to the wall and told him to keep his mouth shut and follow orders if he wanted to hold his job. The young manager thought about the potential consequences of resisting change despite fuel costs and found a job in another industry. And Chrysler's small automobile came on the market with an engine and transmission built in Germany because the massive V-8 engine was an anachronism that no one would buy.

The resistance to change that so complicates the work of managers and supervisors is much more than a conscious determination to keep things as they were in the past. According to scholars like Konrad Lorenz and Carl Jung, our resistance may well be rooted in the evolution of humankind, in the development of Western Civilization itself, and in the manner in which work groups have been led in our society.

As our civilization grew in size and complexity, humans developed the technology needed to prosper *and* the interpersonal relationships necessary for success. In other words, our ancestors created both the *hardware* (the resources) and the *software* (the relationships) of achievement. The hardware included tools, weapons, clothes, etc. The software included the psychology and the philosophy needed to work successfully in groups, to distribute rewards equitably, and to avoid unnecessary conflict within each community. We must still balance the use of software and hardware if our organizations are to prosper as our competitors do in Europe and Asia.

In many, if not most, cases, an organization begins as an entrepreneurial enterprise that prospers in that form as long as the founder uses both good hardware and software to serve clients well. In time, the small organization grows beyond the ability of the entrepreneur to control everything, so either the transition to professional management is made or else the company stagnates upon the death of the founder. However, it has only been in the last few decades that we have come to understand that there is a drawback to professionally managed organizations that do not change as society changes.

For example, when an organization becomes so complex that people feel lost in its activities, confused about its objectives, and resentful of its impersonal approach, the organization has peaked. At that point, to become optimally successful, the management team must regain the community spirit that has so frequently been destroyed through the development of impersonal systems, a division of labor, and the rest of the Industrial Engineering/Harvard Business approach.

In communities where men build ships for their sons and nephews to fish in or fight from, quality is *never* a problem. When people are hired to build products—or small parts of products—for a faceless consumer market, *or* for managers they do not know because they are away soaring like falcons in a deserted forest, quality and productivity are *certain* to be consistent problems. And therein hangs a tale for ambitious managers and supervisors who believe there is a better way to work in their organizations.

One Measure of Success

Business has become too complex to believe that profit alone is the measure of how well an organization is serving its clients and utilizing its employees. Joseph Juran, the quality specialist who, with W. Edwards Deming, gave Japan the tools they needed to prosper with small inventories in their production organizations, has blamed our leadership failure on the finance specialists of our organizations. In their pursuit of short-term profit, they neglected the quality and productivity that would have created long-range growth for their organizations. In all fairness, the finance wizards were only doing what their owners hired them to do, and since they seldom had any production or service experience, our performance calamity caught them unawares. Unfortunately, the belief that the bottom line rather than growth is crucial was accepted by the smaller organizations of our society as well.

A more reliable measure of success that far transcends the quarterly statement is a manager's ability to increase productivity and quality enough to capture more of the market without a proportional increase in expenses. Scholars like David Tansik, Edwin Flippo, and Peter Drucker report that we have probably come as far as possible without a restoration of creativity—a rebirth of the human element in our organizations.

We must remember that we suffered our massive leadership failure while using the best administrative systems ever devised. We neglected the human relationships that are so valuable because they seemed less reliable and certainly more troublesome than inanimate systems, while our less sophisticated competitors around the world harnessed the human strengths that can make any organization strong and vibrant—and productive!

Fortunately, the behavioral sciences, especially the research of psychology and sociology, have matured past traditional concepts to identify and teach methods that can restore to any organization the achievement that it needs. An entire nation—Japan—did just that. Men and women at all levels of responsibility worked very hard to reach what first seemed to be impossible goals. I think that the time has now come when a great many Western managers are willing to learn how to better lead their organizations to productivity and quality.

To succeed in today's business climate, each manager must best utilize the organization's hardware and software to produce goods or services that will continue on the market. This means that few companies will become optimally successful without a conscious dedication to service through its people. To do that well will require that each manager and supervisor learn as much as possible about human personality, productivity, and motivation and use the new concepts effectively.

A Loss of Power

Some organizations have prospered through the use of interpersonal power—with the sheer authority to insist that employees or members do as they are told—but they are now a vanishing breed. In a free society, the exercise of personal power over employees was never a very good way for managers to succeed, although in a simple time the *means* of production were often confused with the *ends* of commitment and cooperation. The use of power to insure profits and growth was never a very efficient means, though it was widely used at a time when jobs were scarce, tasks were simple, and people had been socialized to obey politely from the day they were born.

In a simple, hand-to-mouth world, as ours was when the Industrial Revolution established the practices still blindly followed by many in management, power may have been a fair way to keep the peasant pulling plows and scaling castle walls amid showers of stones and flaming oil. However, in our age of change, when young people are no longer programmed to respond to managerial demands with a tug at the forelock and a polite "by your leave, sir," the use of power rather than persuasion and participation is the worst possible method of trying to reach any organization's objectives.

Most importantly, the use of power no longer works. Only when punishment is an ever-present threat can people be forced to repress their individuality. In an affluent, politically free society, where people have vast surpluses of food, fossil energy sources, and sophisticated technology, the use of interpersonal power is completely counterproductive. Workers simply elect officials who enact statutes to protect their constituents. The court systems assure people freedom from most managerial power. So do union contracts. The most important factor of all, however, is the shift in employee expectations. Every successful organization in the world succeeds because the rank-and-file members quietly and without fanfare do what needs to be done. And now, employees have a radically different set of expectations of their companies.

In the past, when the barons of production had the economic and political power to demand employee compliance, they worked through men and women who were trained to obey. The workers of that era were reared in stern homes where the fathers were dominant figures. They attended hickory-stick schools in which the desks were bolted in rows to the floor. Their pastors were authoritarian men who thundered about God's wrath toward slothful people. Everyone *had* to work hard, for only through incessant labor could starvation be avoided next winter!

That all changed in this century with the widespread use of fossil fuels that created a great surplus and the affluence we now have. With human labor replaced by machines, fathers had time to mellow and play with their children. Schools abandoned the traditional teaching of the 3 Rs by rote instruction in favor of complex subjects that required active participation. Religious leaders started conducting encounter groups, and police departments offered courses in human relationships. Virtually every institution in our society, except for business, has given up on an authoritarian approach to dealing with men and women. As of now, virtually no one has the power to dominate employees.

A participant in the Executive Development Conference at the University of Arizona manages a copper smelter in a western state. One evening we discussed his loss of power to demand compliance in his community. For several decades, he said, he was considered a pillar of stability and progress in the city. His capital and work brought jobs, prosperity, and affluence to the employees and the merchants who served the community. He had only to endorse a political candidate to have people take him seriously. Real-estate agents sought his favor, and the police never ticketed his automobile. He had power and he used it wisely, he assured me.

That all changed as power became more and more diffused among different groups in the city. A growing number of teachers, pastors, and politicians began calling him an exploiter of the land. County commissioners no longer ask his opinion on new developments, and a growing movement among the people is forcing him to buy expensive pollution control equipment even though his low-grade ore and antiquated plant may make it unprofitable. If he does what other power brokers demand, his business may fail, but if he does not, he will be harassed by court injunctions that will probably force him to close his smelter. He simply does not have the power to work as he did in the past. He is not alone, as many managers admit when I question them.

One of the worst things that a manager can do, when clinging to an antiquated concept of productivity and success, is to pretend that interpersonal power is still held by managers when it is not. The pretense of power, like most other mistaken assumptions, leads to making decisions that harm their organizations. Men and women seem, too often, to confuse prestige and privilege with power. They accept corner offices, reserved parking places, and decorated dining rooms, but they receive the performance that the employees collectively grant them. And in the many companies where the pretense of power limits the esteem and commitment of the workers, the workers have not been especially generous to short-sighted managers. In fact, they have skinned them and hung their scalps out to dry!

Interpersonal Success

When I speak to business and professional groups, I find an increasing number of men and women who are seeking more effective ways of understanding the cultural revolution occurring in Western Civilization, who want the commitment and cooperation they can win with employee trust and respect. Some of the managers have read Eric Hoffer, the longshoreman philosopher, who wrote that most people find it more important to be needed than to be affluent or powerful. Hoffer spent decades of his life laboring as a freight handler in the mornings and as a writer on the human condition in the afternoons. He wrote, and I agree completely with him, that people need a sense of purpose in their relationships and on their jobs.

History is filled with examples of ragged, tatter-demalion groups that achieved a great deal because their leaders gave them respect, an opportunity to win self-esteem, and first-class citizenship in a surrogate community of achievers. The slaves rebelling with Spartacus, Queen Anne's tattered guard, Lee's barefoot Confederates double-timing 14 miles to Sharpsburg, and skinny little Vietnamese riflemen shivering with malaria in the monsoon before Tet—all knew why they were there, that they were needed, and that their contributions were honored. So do the workers at Harmon, Dana, Coors Brewery, and a growing number of companies in which the managers have chosen productivity as it must be won from employees in this new area of shared power.

Productivity can reach optimal levels only when the people managing an organization develop lasting reasons for the employees to give their best efforts. Serious commitment will always remain the by-product of supportive relationships and challenging activities that are connected to the organization's objectives. The most successful managers will consistently connect an effective use of organizational *hardware* to the sophisticated utilization of the groups' *software*—its committed people.

I have found, from my research in many organiza-

13

tions, that the process of creating a community of achievers that rewards managers typically moves through these four stages:

Confusion: This follows the assumption that a manager can succeed, despite the changes of our era, with the age-old method of purchasing the workers' time with wages, assigning appropriate tasks, and punishing the people who do not comply with demands made upon them. In this stage of managerial effectiveness, employees are penalized or replaced when they protest being excluded from the important aspects of organizational life. When conflicts arise because employees are being led in ways that were abandoned by the family, school, and church, and when productivity no longer increases, confusion and resentment mount. Executives put pressure on managers, managers harass supervisors, and supervisors, who are always caught in the middle, insult their employees. CEOs are replaced so rapidly that they have no time to redirect their organizations; middle managers retire on the job but don't leave; and employees become adversaries who don't want to help the supervisors they believe are causing them to lose their self-esteem by denying them the right to become first-class citizens of the group.

Communication: This aspect of growth toward organizational maturity begins when its leaders look beyond traditional ways to seek better methods for improving the group's software. People are encouraged to question things that have remained negative and limiting to group members. New management skills are learned and used to express productive attitudes and expectations through new channels of communication. The entire process of communication is revised to include *listening* by managers as well as *telling* what should be accomplished. A special effort is made to include more men and women in the leadership and decision-making process so the adversary relationship soon lessens. At this stage of growth, many of the employees remain cautious and uncommitted. They fear it is a maneuver to gain an advantage over them, to win greater productivity without any share in the rewards of their effort.

Cooperation: In this stage, an organization's executives and managers have convinced the employees, through deeds and attitudes, that they are esteemed, first-class citizens of the organization. Their contributions will be rewarded consistently, and they shall receive an equitable proportion of the payoffs that the company earns. At this point, the majority of the group is ready to listen to new ideas, for trust has been established, a philosophy of service is understood, and the desire to be useful among one's peers is being cultivated. The adversary relationship that cripples so many companies is being negated by the satisfaction of mutual achievement.

Commitment: When an organization reaches this point, using effective mutual communication to win cooperation consistently, the stage is set to gain broad-based commitment from the employees. The work group has become a surrogate community in which the achievers know that the hardware will be used to support people, rather than people being used and abused for the good of the hardware. The adversary relationship has vanished as company leadership persuades people to work well in a team effort because the managers prefer productivity, profits, and growth to personal perogatives and power that destroy employee commitment.

I have never taught that it is easy to move through this process to create a community of achievers. If it were, the productivity of the English-speaking world would not be in shambles. It took Richard Harmon of Harmon International four years of hard work to develop the level of trust that he wanted when he assumed leadership of the family organization. However, by any standard, it was worth it. Labor contracts are signed months in advance. Jobs that took two and three days are completed in one day. Productivity and quality are improving constantly. Harmon International is not alone.

According to quality and productivity specialists Juran and Deming, a planned program to follow Harmon's example will lead to a 33% reduction of labor costs with the same level of productivity, a 66% reduction in inventory requirements, and a 25% reduction in floor or manufacturing space. A manufacturing company with such an approach can function with a two-hour inventory and be secure.

One electronics firm spent about a quarter of a million dollars developing quality and performance teams to gain a reduction of waste from three million to one million dollars annually. As Philip Crosby writes, *Quality Is Free* but it isn't easy to come by. The feeling of achievement is a human need, but many organizations have so crippled the growth of the rank-and-file members that they don't hold the emotional ownership of the group's challenges and rewards.

There is one question that comes up in almost every seminar I conduct. It seems inevitable that someone will ask why a management team or an individual manager should make the effort to win the cooperation and commitment of the employees. Is it not fair that the employees do as they are told because they are being paid for their work? Yes, I am forced to answer, it is fair. When we take the King's shilling, we follow his drummer—in theory at least. That, however, does not change the fact that some regiments are much better organized and led, year after year, than other regiments. For, as Napoleon stated, there are no bad regiments—only bad colonels. Tradition has it that Napoleon also said that with enough medals, he could conquer the world. While that was an overstatement, as he found out at Waterloo, he did understand the importance of first-class membership in the organization, respect that flowed both ways, and self-esteem for the rank and file.

Frederick Herzberg set the record straight about the use of pay to win commitment with his two-factor theory. He wrote, very perceptively, that new employees feel they must earn their pay—*for about two weeks after coming on the job*. After they are accepted by their peers, a subtle change takes place. They feel at home in the group and unconsciously expect their pay *as a result of belonging to the work group*. In a fragile society, the pay was enough. In an affluent age, the entire process has changed, and managers must work on a different level of motivation in order to succeed.

Motivation in Organizations

Motivation, in work-centered organizations, is never something one person does *to* another. *It is an internal, extremely personal movement toward some goal that can be described in the inevitable fact that people alone or in groups consistently do whatever is important to themselves.* Because personality is complex and behavior often symbolic in nature, the movement toward personal goals is frequently subtle and convoluted enough to confuse a manager. But under the enormous amount of symbolism to which humans are inclined, a fairly simple model of motivation emerges. It is this:

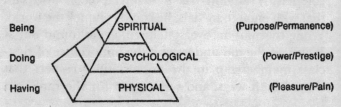

Being	SPIRITUAL	(Purpose/Permanence)
Doing	PSYCHOLOGICAL	(Power/Prestige)
Having	PHYSICAL	(Pleasure/Pain)

The pyramid can be considered an extension of the personality into the real world of work, love, worship, and play. Each aspect of motivation affects a person's depth of commitment according to the personality traits possessed. I have created this model to deliberately follow the historic progression of psychology from 1880 to 1980. It also follows the progression of brain/mind functions at higher and higher levels. From the medula up through the cortex, the processes of life become more and more complex as does motivation for our intelligent, creative species when we are not stifled with emotional repression.

Motivation begins with the Pleasure/Pain Principle. Few people would deny that normal individuals prefer pleasure to suffering pain in the classic reinforcement system formulated by Sigmund Freud and refined by B.F. Skinner. In this largely *physical* aspect of motivation, people are usually moved to *have* what they can obtain through their skill or knowledge. Food, shelter, transportation, and entertaining distractions form some of the *having* needs that motivate men and women. Many people work at routine, demeaning jobs for humiliating managers in order to feed, clothe, and educate their children. But in a civilization where the typical worker is more affluent than a Mandarin emperor, it is too much to expect any great depth of commitment from a system that rewards people only in the physical aspects of personality.

In the psychological aspect of motivation, men and women behave according to the Power/Prestige Principle first discussed by Alfred Adler and refined in greater detail by Eric Berne in transactional analysis. More than half a century ago, Adler realized that Freud's rather simple concept of motivation couldn't account for the way humans committed themselves to laborious or even painful activities or why they continued striving to achieve more after they were affluent. It *is* difficult, using the Pleasure/Pain Principle of motivation, to explain why so many North Vietnamese infantrymen conducted their own funerals before marching hundreds of miles through leech-infested jungles to attack a powerful mechanized enemy.

Adler wrote that we all need prestige and self-esteem in order to feel good about ourselves and to continue our cooperation with a group. So it is. After the having needs are met, consistently, normal people look for challenging things to *do* as a means of enhancing their lives and gaining self-esteem. Our *doing* needs become paramount after the having needs are regularly being met.

In the third aspect of motivation, the typical person moves to the Purpose/Permanence Principle first alluded to by Viktor Frankl and then developed in greater detail by myself in my *Search For Meaning* seminar and research. In this final aspect of motivation, after each person's physical and psychological requirements are met consistently, the *spiritual* dimension of life becomes dominant. This is the need to *become* what a person has the capacity to become. And any organization which does not facilitate the development of its people to this aspect of life and work cannot reach its potential. Men and women want to become what they can be, as a means of contributing best and as a means of gaining self-esteem, so any manager who frustrates this growth is handicapping the organization.

This progression is a sign of good health, though

the three major aspects of motivation are as mixed as the ingredients of a cake after it has been baked. Consider an attempt to motivate employees in the physical aspects of personality and motivation alone. How many steak dinners can a normal person eat before the sight of another one becomes repulsive? Taken to the extreme, how many luxury automobiles can you park in front of your home before another one no longer moves you to commitment? Yet, disturbed men and women often gorge themselves into obesity because their motivation is centered around having food rather than going on to other aspects of life and service. The same principle of satiation follows in the psychological aspects of motivation. When a society frees itself from scarcity, many people become bored and are no longer motivated greatly by doing the same job for the rest of their lives. Thus, in our era, the typical person changes careers several times, looking for greener pastures and bigger challenges.

Unfortunately, a majority of organizations freeze their official attempts to win employee commitment at the lowest level—in the physical aspects of motivation. Managers offer a welder, who is making 10 dollars an hour, a 50 cent an hour raise, but deny him the opportunity to participate in any decisions of importance and wonder why he remains uncommitted. Changing markets and circumstances put the leaders under pressure; a very common response is to start *taking numbers and kicking arse*. Finally, entire organizations and industries become infantile and neurotic as people put in their time, give up on achieving together, take their pay, and withhold commitment. No one can motivate another person, since motivation wells up from within; but we certainly cannot win anyone's commitment with an antiquated approach to management when people are afloat on a sea of affluence. Sensory satiation prohibits it.

To understand how satiation can be avoided in an organization, invert the pyramid of motivation. The model then looks like this:

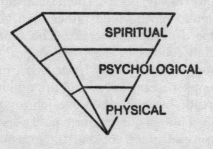

In the physical aspects of motivation, we have very little capacity before we are satiated and no longer moved to work hard. In the psychological aspects, each person's capacity to achieve is greater before satiation and dissatisfaction set in. In the final aspect, at the spiritual or open-ended aspect of motivation, satiation seldom occurs. It shouldn't, for at this level people are maturing and becoming more and more competent and valuable to themselves, to their peers, and to their organizations.

Men and women who lead others must capitalize on the innate human needs to *have*, to *do*, and to *become* by managing their groups so people consistently win *pleasure* rather than *pain* at the *physical* level, *prestige* and *esteem* rather than *devaluation* at the *psychological* level, and *purpose* and *permanence* rather than *meaninglessness* at the *spiritual* level. When this view of how and why people are moved to cooperate with people they trust is integrated into the activities and attitudes of managers, great things are possible in an individual's career.

2

Patterns And Management

Centuries ago, in the Golden Age of Greece, Socrates tried to develop a system for understanding the attitudes of men and women while predicting the way they would act in their relationships with others. Evidently, he considered it important, even then, for people who were responsible for the labor of others to work through the individual differences of their followers. Much later in the scheme of history, a Swiss psychologist named Carl G. Jung developed yet another system for understanding people well enough to influence their contributions in the home and on the job. Finally, starting in the 1950s, a number of American psychologists actually began conducting research into social styles or personality patterns that could help perceptive managers and supervisors work more effectively with people as they actually are.

As I work in many organizations and teach an unending series of classes with managers, I am convinced that we have come as far as we can by systematizing and objectifying our organizations. The time has come, in our day, to subjectify our leadership, to draw men and women together into the kind of organization that William Ouchi calls a Theory Z company, into a team effort that I call a Community of Achievers. I have already mentioned some very sound organizations that work and produce effectively because they accept and harness the needs that people feel rather than having their employees adapt to inadequate company requirements.

In the past half century, when psychologists were struggling to be accepted as objective, rigorous scientists—precisely as chemists and biologists were objective scientists—many researchers did managers a great disservice. They rejected the subjective human element of loyalty, commitment, attitudes, and personality in a quest for constant objectivity so that people could be programmed and utilized as reliably as the equipment. They said again and again, to any executive, manager, or supervisor who was so naive as to listen, that only behavior mattered. So long as a person completed his or her quota, as long as the behavior met standards, all would be well.

However, times changed, and we found ourselves being pressed harder by organizations around the world that were concerned with those intangibles that we frequently rejected because of our naive beliefs that only behavior counted. Our Asian and European competitors talked about employee participation, esteem, cooperation, and commitment. They discussed—without embarrassment—ethics, values, trust, attitudes, and expectations that were forbidden to American managers by peer pressure for many decades. Then a growing number of management/productivity researchers and practitioners banded together to investigate the real world of productivity and growth in commercial organizations.

Thus, I wrote *Nice Guys Finish First, The Leadership Seminar, The Self-Profile*, and developed my *Productivity Improvement System* to deal with the need to harness human traits in a new manner if we are to profit and grow in our companies. Each of these deals with the personality patterns that people bring to their organizations, patterns that managers must understand and utilize in order to maximize productivity while maintaining the trust and cooperation of the employees. It seems to many now, as my materials are used around the world from Stockholm to Singapore, from Mexico City to Tokyo and Saudi Arabia, that these concepts are extremely useful to managers in all kinds of organizations. Because of that I should review them for the reader's benefit.

Each person's personality pattern is formed early in life through a combination of inherited traits, learned experiences, and personal choices until, by the age of four or five, each person clearly demonstrates the pattern he or she shall use through life. For example, I have one grandchild who is now eight. Melanie is a quick-thinking youngster who *asks* me for little. Instead, she *tells* me what I can do for her in a dominant, directive manner. Her cousin, Aaron, is four, and he is a laughing, running clown who demonstrates with great glee his skill on a tricycle or rocking horse. He already demonstrates extroverted personality traits that Melanie does not have. Baby Rachel, another cousin of theirs and my youngest grandchild, is a thoughtful, cautious little girl of 14 months who already shows signs of thinking things through before making a decision.

Each maturing child blends together traits, experiences, and choices in such a way that he or she feels comfortable dealing with life and others. If this process of personality development is drawn as a simple equation, it looks like this:

$$P = f(H \times E \times C)$$

Personality equals the function of heredity, multiplied by environment, multiplied by all the choices that a person makes during the formative years. Therefore, a person whose personality equation includes $P = f(H^{13} \times E^8 \times C^{17})$ will certainly be different from one whose personality equation includes $P = f(H^{11} \times E^{19} \times C^{22})$.

Furthermore, there is nothing a manager can do about it. The elements of personality are set and jelled years or even decades before the person appears on the job as an adult.

Patterns at Work

In one organization that I consult, everyone knows that Thomas, the founding dentist, will consistently deal with everyone in a blunt, outspoken manner that leaves little time for personal amenities. He is sober, to the point, and quickly becomes impatient with people who ask too many questions when he is making assignments. The employees also know that Thomas is absolutely fair when it comes to raises and promotions, never criticizes anyone in secret, and is willing to help anyone who asks for advice. He is a good leader, has the staff well organized, and can be relied on at all times.

Walter, another dentist who came into the practice later, works from a low-key style that maintains a friendly network of employees. Everyone likes him, enjoys his chatting between tasks, and confides in him about their personal problems and concerns. Despite the way that he always seems to have time to share a friendly word with others, his productivity actually runs ahead of Thomas's in the average month.

Anne, the office manager, is a happy, extroverted woman who does not fit the pattern that many people assign to managers. She does her job well, is accepted by the staff as an integral member of the team, and keeps the atmosphere cheery despite the usual patient fears of dental services. Anne has told me how Thomas draws her back to reality when she soars into flights of extravagant rhetoric. *He* has told me how he appreciates the way she lightens the emotional load since he cannot do it himself. They both say that their friendship with Walter is a cherished part of their lives.

In other words, despite their personality pattern differences, the three people have come to trust, respect, and rely upon each other as a community of achievers that works well together. These people, and the employees who work with them, draw from each other's strengths and contributions. While a company can succeed and make money, it will never reach its ultimate potential unless the managers learn enough about the employees and themselves to create an emotional climate that transcends employee compliance to orders.

Each person functions best from what I call the Comfort Zone. This zone is the span of attitudes, expectations, and acts that allows a person to accomplish the greatest amount of work for the smallest expenditure of psychic and physical energy. People function best with a degree of tension that compels them to work toward worthwhile goals, but this productivity peaks when the tension becomes counterproductive stress. When a person is pressed out of the Comfort Zone by someone with the wit or power to do so, he or she spends too much time dealing with pressures instead of working wisely and well.

Each person should, furthermore, be judged while he and the judge are both in their Comfort Zones. To make a decision about a person when he or she is under stress is to overlook the fact that the behavior and attitudes are not typical at such a time. To judge another person while *you* are under stress is to overlook the fact that your judgment is severely skewed and that you are in an emotional, egocentric bind. Seldom do good decisions occur when managers are under such stress that they are not interpreting relationships and events as they really are.

Pattern Origins

In my research (some 50,000 people have been measured with my *Self-Profile*), I have found that people interact according to two major personality trends. First of all, each person has what psychologists commonly call the *fight-or-flight syndrome*. In stressful situations, we try to survive or at least prosper by either attacking threatening situations and people or fleeing them. In our aeons of development as fangless, thin-skinned little creatures, we learned the two basic survival skills. The first was to flee as fast and as far as possible since a tiger couldn't eat you if it couldn't catch you. The other tactic was to attack violently since the tiger couldn't eat you if it was being eaten. For countless centuries, our ancestors survived with these two methods and passed the traits on to their children. Finally, today, we still have them although they are concealed and modified with some degree of sophistication in our organizations.

There is another aspect of personality pattern development that every manager should know. It is just as critical as the fight-or-flight tendency. The second personality trend is the *conceal-or-reveal syndrome*. Each person, as he or she combines inherited traits, environmental experiences, and personal choices [the $P = f(H \times E \times C)$ equation] learns that it is sometimes wise to hide feelings from others and sometimes best to reveal them. Just as one cannot succeed in business by clouting the boss over the head, neither can a person succeed by blurting out everything that is felt. On the other hand, one cannot build a

strong team by running screaming from the office
when frustrated, nor can one win employee commitment by remaining poker-faced while the employees
try to guess one's feelings.

In civilized societies as well as in organizations that
are well managed, the fight-or-flight tendency has
become *competition and cooperation* along a horizontal
line. Some people *compete* to control the conversation,
the choices, the use of resources, and the activities.
Other people are much more comfortable *cooperating*
in their interpersonal relationships. When the data
are plotted for a great number of people, this
compete-or-cooperate shifting of the fight-or-flight
syndrome forms a continuum from very competitive
to highly cooperative. The distribution looks like this:

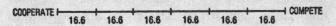

COOPERATE ├────┼────┼────┼────┼────┼────┤ COMPETE
       16.6   16.6   16.6   16.6   16.6   16.6

About 16.6% of all normal men and women fit
naturally into each division. The closer to either edge,
the more pronounced the cooperative or competitive
tendencies are in a person's attitudes and acts. Cooperative people appear thoughtful of others, unwilling to make abrupt decisions, and willing to negotiate
their activities. Competitive people appear more
outspoken, swift in making decisions, and dominant
in relationships and negotiations. I am referring to
interpersonal relationships here, not about the desire
to excel in business, the professions, athletics, or a
life task *and* I shall return to that distinction later.

All my research reveals that there is no best or
worst place to be on the continuum, except for being

so close to the edge that you cannot relate to or accept people who have traits different from your own. When that is the case, as it was for Coach Vincent Lombardi of the Green Bay Packers, crucial interpersonal problems are created for the organization. For, regardless of which of the four primary patterns you have, three-fourths of the human race will have different patterns. And in a management setting, it is extremely unlikely that all employees—to say nothing of customers—have been selected to fit a preconceived pattern.

However, some organizations have, unfortunately, fallen into the trap of believing that only managers with certain personality patterns are effective. One large paper products company suffered horrendous financial losses when it absorbed a smaller company that had equally strong beliefs that only its pattern was right for a business company. The men clashed continually and little was accomplished, for both groups felt the other was wrong. Another large insurance company that I worked with believed that only interpersonally competitive people were successful in selling insurance. The managers developed an incentive program that satisfied their personality needs, invested millions of dollars in it, and were astonished to find that three-fourths of their rank-and-file people cared little for it.

The conceal-or-reveal syndrome is modified to include the self-control or self-express traits that all people have. In a vertical distribution, it looks like this:

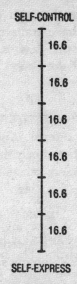

SELF-CONTROL

16.6

16.6

16.6

16.6

16.6

16.6

SELF-EXPRESS

Once more, the distribution is from one extreme to the other, from rigid, poker-face self-discipline on the top to a babbling of virtually everything one feels at the other. Neither extreme is good for a manager, since either will confuse and alienate employees. Within the normal range, however, there is no best trait to have. According to my research, self-controlled and self-expressed people are successful in all areas of life and leadership, so long as they use their own traits well to win the commitment and cooperation of their followers. Once again, however, some organizations have favorite styles that place managers and employees at a disadvantage if they do not have the approved style.

By combining the two data distributions, the following chart emerges:

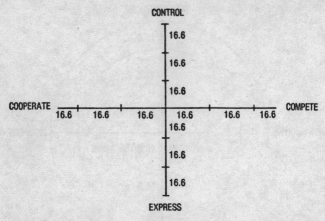

The scores from my *Self-Profile* create this chart of personality characteristics. The people who fit evenly into the inner circle have their traits to a lesser degree while those who protrude unevenly into the outer circle have those traits more strongly. As can be seen from the figure below, there are *four* primary personality patterns. They are the Controlling, the Entertaining, the Supporting, and the Comprehending patterns.

The *Controlling* personality pattern is that used by men and women who combine the tendency to use self-control and to compete interpersonally with others. These people, who tend to think of themselves as *Self-Reliant*, are assertive and dominant in their relationships, not given to joking or telling stories, and not overly concerned with the emotions of others. They are the *Command* specialists of life who remain in their Comfort Zones by *telling other people what to do*. Henry Ford and Henry Ford II

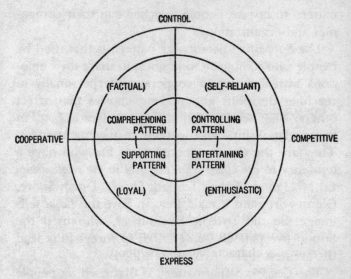

both had Controlling personality patterns, as did John Wayne. Billy Graham, Bella Abzug, and Richard Nixon also fall into this group. Like the other three, this *Self-Reliant* self-image is completely normal, and many people become effective managers by using it well.

The *Entertaining* personality pattern is that used by people who combine a willingness to compete interpersonally with a tendency to express what they feel. These are the men and women who see themselves as *Enthusiastic* in their relationships and at the tasks they work to complete. They are the *Emotive* specialists of society and life who remain in their Comfort Zones by *telling others what they feel*. Johnny Carson, Joan Rivers, and Beverly Sills have this pattern. So did Lyndon Johnson. Many excellent leaders use this pattern to inspire people to achieve in their companies and organizations.

The *Supporting* personality pattern is that used by people who combine a willingness to share their emotions with a desire to cooperate interpersonally in reaching decisions and making choices that affect others. They tend to think of themselves as *Loyal* in their relationships and in their management styles. They are the *Concern* specialists of life who have a tendency to *ask others what they feel in the relationship*. Ed McMahon of the "Tonight Show," Dinah Shore, Glenn Ford, and Ronald Reagan have this *Loyal* self-image. So did Dwight Eisenhower, who used the Supportive pattern well enough to successfully lead the greatest military coalition in history.

The *Comprehending* pattern is that used by people who combine a willingness to cooperate interpersonally with others and a desire to maintain control of their own emotions. These people often think of themselves as *Factual* in their management styles and their relationships. They are the *Information* specialists of society and are most comfortable discovering pertinent facts before reaching decisions. They have a common tendency to *ask others what they are doing* in order to remain in their Comfort Zones. Jimmy Stewart, Eric Sevareid, Katharine Hepburn, and Jimmy Carter have a *Factual* self-image or a Comprehending personality pattern.

Without a doubt, people with the Controlling, Entertaining, Supporting, and Comprehending patterns can all be equally effective as managers *if* they have the maturity to use their styles effectively while accepting and rewarding people who are different from themselves. If, however, they accept some organization's myth that only one certain pattern (usually Controlling) is effective in management, they will become a part of Western Civilization's leadership failure.

Pattern Weakness

One fascinating factor I find in pattern research is the way that the strengths of a particular pattern become weaknesses if pressed too far. For example, a Controller who plunges ahead with the emotionless use of systems and objective procedures because he or she feels especially Self-Reliant may well come to grief when the employees need support or warmth that is not given. Then, when the Controller needs extra effort in times of stress, the employees do not commit themselves because the manager has remained a distant, cool figure.

Few people have demonstrated how strengths become weaknesses more clearly than Henry Ford II. As a young man who assumed leadership of The Ford Motor Company when he was only 29 years old, Ford surrounded himself with men with whom he felt at ease. Since the young executive was near the outer limit of the chart as a high interpersonal risk, dominant Controller, he chose few introspective, analytic subordinates for his management team. Robert McNamara and Lee Iacocca are but two of the executives who were like peas in a pod with young Ford in those early years of his tenure in the company that his grandfather founded.

For some reason, possibly because his own father, Edsel Ford, was unable to please the founder of the firm, Henry II decided that only Controllers, with whom he felt comfortable, were capable of leading others successfully. He evidently was not introspective enough, or sufficiently sophisticated in psychology, to recognize that many other firms have leaders with other patterns. The company came close to disaster because the management team was not introspective enough to discover what was going on in the emotions of the people who buy automobiles.

Ford's personality pattern, which included such strengths as determination, fortitude, and courage, backfired when it was not balanced by flexibility and cooperation. According to Bill Moyers in his *Journal*, when more perceptive executives wanted to build small, competitive automobiles to meet the Asian Challenge, Ford snorted in disgust and declared that if the American people wanted economy in their cars, he would see that they paid through the nose for it. He cut the research and development budget for fuel-efficient automobiles by 75%, and the survival of his company is in doubt to this day. Of course, he is no longer running the company after such a terrible misdirection of his competitive and controlling pattern.

Controllers, and their *Self-Reliant* self-images, often fail when they court risks that could be minimized with research and when they ignore the emotions of the people who must do the work that makes any organization productive.

Entertainers, with their *Enthusiastic* self-images, often fail because their undeniable strength of many interests causes them to venture into new areas before completing current tasks. They may assume that a task is being handled correctly because they have creatively conceived it. And while a good conversational ability is a strength, it becomes a weakness if used so much that it blocks valuable input from other people.

Supporters excel at leading people of different patterns and conflicting ambitions to work well together. *Loyals* sometimes get into trouble, however, by continuing to accept diverse opinions and negotiations when the time has come to settle into a single course of action.

Comprehenders, with their *Factual* self-images, are ideal at digging out information needed to make good management decisions. That is far better than leaping blindly at assumptions without any verification. When, however, Comprehenders continue to survey all the available data and then ask for more, the strength becomes a weakness. In the quick and dirty world of work, a manager must often make decisions before much of the desired data is available. Otherwise, the decision is made for the manager by default.

Pattern Utilization

When organizing a team effort, consider the following factors when selecting people to work well toward goals.

Comprehenders serve best by carefully investigating and analyzing information. They search and discover from their *concept* orientation. Place people with strong, Factual self-images in jobs that need those research and analysis skills.

Controllers serve best by boldly implementing and directing activities. They select and solve problems from their *action* orientation. Place people with Self-Reliant self-images in jobs where they can make bold decisions.

Entertainers serve most effectively by inspiring and reinforcing positive activities. They persuade people to give appropriate performances from their *inspiring* orientation. Place people with sound, Enthusiastic self-images in jobs where excitement and stimulation are good for the task.

Supporters serve best by educating and counseling others. They help people develop their skills to reach their potential from their *agreement* orientation. Utilize people with strong, Loyal self-images in situations where negotiation and compromise are essential.

Any leader who accepts only one pattern as effective, because he or she is interested primarily in remaining in his Comfort Zone, is crippling the work team. Collectively, men and women have different strengths and can move any sound organization to a higher level of productivity and effectiveness by using these strengths wisely and well.

Pattern Conflicts

Many of the unnecessary conflicts in organizations stem from the inflexible belief of some people that only one pattern is useful and that others have to adopt it. When *Nice Guys Finish First* came out, a personal friend of mine read it and called me immediately to report that he understood, for the first time in 16 years, why he had so many conflicts with one of the deans in his college. We talked for a while and then he asked, rather ruefully, if I had any suggestions about how to get his dean to read the book.

The majority of pattern conflicts occur diagonally across the chart. For example, Controllers and Entertainers share competitiveness, which gives them a basis for mutual understanding. Entertainers and Supporters share self-expression, which also helps them understand each other. Controllers and Supporters share none of the crucial traits; neither do Entertainers and Comprehenders. This makes it harder to develop understanding in their relationships. Because they do not share the same emotions, they may misunderstand each other's motives and values.

I recently consulted in an organization where the conflict between an action-oriented physician with a strong Controlling pattern and a soft-spoken agreement-oriented physician with a Supporting pattern seriously compromised the effectiveness of the group. As I talked to the men, I soon found that both physicians unconsciously assumed that his own pattern was normal and that the other was wrong. They failed completely to see that they were both reacting negatively because each was being forced out of his Comfort Zone. Both physicians were too rigid to adapt and completely ignorant about personality patterns. One man told me:

> That man is crazy. He wants to control and manage everything we do. He thinks that by directing every detail of the practice, our income will increase. He ignores the suggestions of our assistants, cares nothing about our feelings, and orders me about like I was one of the hired hands. At times I go out of my way to set him off, because afterwards he'll hide and sulk for about a week.

However, his partner had another opinion:

> That man is a wimp. He never takes the responsibility for telling the staff what to do, wastes too much time asking them what they feel, and humors the patients too long. If he would act like a real doctor, tell people what they need to do, and move along faster, we would have no more problems here. He is just too weak to run a good office.

Many organizations have that problem to some degree. While few of them actually lose a fortune because of it, one major New England insurance company did. A team of managers, probably working from their own desire to remain in their Comfort Zones, decided that only men and women with Self-Reliant self-images made good insurance salespeople. Employment tests and interviews were unconsciously slanted to identify and accept only Controllers. It was a disaster; the company spent millions of dollars before discovering that too high a percentage of clients bought insurance and then canceled it when the next payment came due. My research showed that the outer-limit Controllers, with whom company executives were comfortable, were unable to work well with the 80% or more people who were different from themselves.

The Controlling men and women were *demanding* that clients buy insurance. Some would not, of course, but a good percentage did because of the domination of the agent with the Self-Reliant self-image. Then, three months later, the pressured client quietly took revenge and canceled the policy. If you want to avoid problems like this, think about balancing your work team so that all four clusters of strengths are utilized.

Patterns Under Stress

When a person experiences stress, he or she is forced from his Comfort Zone. This usually occurs with some degree of frustration and resentment, of course. I do not mean that tension is wrong—it isn't. Tension is often the simple realization that something must be accomplished within a time limit. Few organizations would accomplish much, were not the managers and employees aware that something must be completed either cooperatively or competitively. No manager can succeed without cultivating the ability to produce task-tension that is directed toward common goals within the organization. Tension is normal, however, until it crosses over and becomes stress that requires more energy than the work itself. The relationship between stress and tension, either in a person's life or in an organization, looks like this:

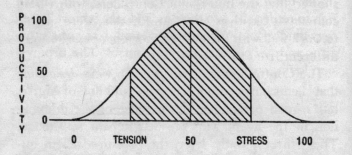

As tension increases to the optimal (the shaded part of the chart), productivity increases also. When pressure increases, however, productivity reaches its peak. Finally, too much pressure creates the stress that reduces productivity and causes a collapse where no work is done at all. The distribution pictured above shows the tapering off of productivity.

When a person moves from the Comfort Zone to tension and stress, several major behavioral changes occur that are consistent with his or her pattern. At times, these shifts will come quickly when the personal involvement is great, thus catching a manager off guard. However, most changes can be predicted, so that a person who understands the shifts for what they are has time to adapt. People shift their behavior in an attempt to return to their Comfort Zones.

By helping them to be rid of excessive tension or stress, you can manage people more effectively. The shifts do remain constant with the fight-or-flight and the conceal-or-reveal syndromes, however.

People with Controlling patterns who are in their Comfort Zones tend to tell others what to do. When under tension, they usually become *autocratic*. If that fails to return them to their individual Comfort Zones, they tend to become frustrated enough to *avoid* situations and people they cannot control. The progression looks like this:

SELF-RELIANT	→	TELLS (Comfort Zone)	→	DEMANDS (Tension)	→	AVOIDS (Stress)

People with Entertaining patterns who are in their Comfort Zones tend to tell others what they feel. When under tension, they tend to *attack*. When that fails to solve the problem, they usually *comply* with others as a means of being comfortable once more. The progression looks like this:

ENTHUSIASTIC	→	TELLS (Comfort Zone)	→	ATTACKS (Tension)	→	COMPLIES (Stress)

People with Supporting patterns progress from asking what others are feeling to acquiescing when under tension to *attacking* when stress develops. The progression looks like this:

LOYAL	→	ASKS (Comfort Zone)	→	COMPLIES (Tension)	→	ATTACKS (Stress)

People with Comprehending patterns move from asking what people are doing to *avoiding* situations and people when under tension to becoming *autocratic* when under stress.

FACTUAL	ASKS (Comfort Zone) →	AVOIDS (Tension) →	DEMANDS (Stress)

President Nixon had a Self-Reliant self-image from which he told others what to do during his career in politics. There remain many pictures of him, jaw clenched firmly, staring at the crowd, telling people what to do for him. When problems set in after the Watergate break-in, he went through the progression like any other person with a Controlling pattern who doesn't understand his own behavior. When frustrated enough to become tense, he became autocratic, demanding that the voters trust him despite the circumstances. He said, "I am *not* a crook!" "I will *never* leave this high office which is my mandate from the people!" His Controlling pattern continued in force, but his demanding did not change the reality of the situation and he could not return to his Comfort Zone.

The entire nation expected a horrendous fight before the Senate when this determined president fought impeachment. But though he could maintain iron-willed self-control under tension, he was true to form when his autocratic demands failed to give him relief. Under stress he began avoiding the pain. According to Woodward and Bernstein, he refused to see his attorneys for weeks at a time, deceived them consistently, and refused to meet with the cabinet until Alexander Haig was the acting president of the nation. The reporters state that Nixon began drinking heavily, which is a form of avoidance, and finally, despite his autocratic statements, left abruptly and returned to California. His is a textbook case of how a Controller reacts to stress when he loses control of a situation.

This shifting of behavior patterns is predictable and, therefore, extremely valuable to managers. For example, you can judge how many demands to put on an amiable Supporter before easing so he doesn't explode in anger. If a Comprehender is avoiding a situation or a relationship that must be managed, a little more pressure on him may force decisive action. By using the chart of behavioral shifts according to personality patterns, you can work with rather than against the normal flow of attitudes and acts. You can predict behavior in advance rather than having to react after the fact.

The Personality Pattern Organizer which follows, is useful for identifying the patterns of others and for deciding how to best influence them. The descriptive information outside the circle tells you what to look for when you are identifying other patterns. The inner material is useful in knowing how to influence a person in each of the four primary patterns. Use your knowledge daily until it becomes second nature to you and watch your management skills improve.

By observing an associate or an employee, you can decide whether he has the traits shown and determine which pattern he uses. Then, by going to the suggestions given on the inside of the circle, you can deal with him more effectively and supportively. By treating your employees as they need to be treated to maintain rapport, you can develop a leadership style that transcends your own needs and that also includes strengths from the other three patterns as well.

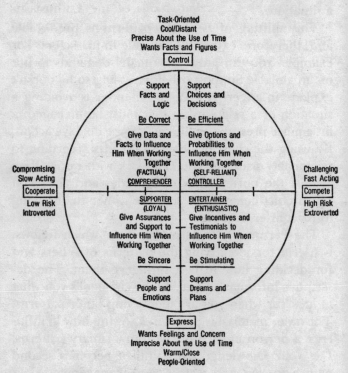

Behaviorial scientists, myself included, have identified the four primary personality patterns discussed in detail in this chapter. Any person's management ability can be greatly improved by drawing together the abilities and skills from across the entire behavioral distribution. By harnessing the task-oriented hardware skills of the Factual and Self-Reliant person into Searching and Discovering, as well as into Implementing and Controlling, a manager can build a solid organization. Then, by drawing together the people-oriented, software skills of the Enthusiastic and Loyal person into Inspiring and Reinforcing and Supporting and Developing employees, a manager can become more successful. When the four approaches are plotted together, they look like this total management approach:

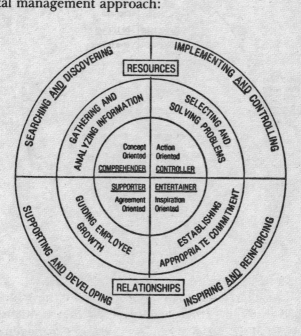

A successful manager improves effectiveness by *gathering and analyzing* information as a *Comprehender* does naturally, progresses to *selecting and solving* problems as a *Controller* does naturally, goes on to *establishing appropriate performance* as an *Entertainer* does naturally, and finally *guides employee growth as a Supporter* does naturally.

There is no more effective way to manage an organization than by combining the task-oriented and human-centered skills that men and women utilize in their organizations.

PART TWO

PERSONALITY PATTERN MANAGEMENT

3

Managing Logically
(Problem Solving)

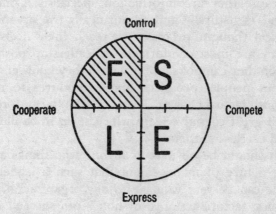

Men and women who combine traits of cooperation and self-control, who see themselves as Factual from their tendency to cooperate and control, have the traits that fit in the upper left section of the Personality Pattern distribution chart. They are the concept-oriented information specialists of life who often appear cool in their relationships, precise about the use of time, and unwilling to accept interpersonal risks. Comprehenders feel all the emotions that more extroverted people do, but they have a natural tendency to keep their feelings hidden from others if they can.

These people who are called Factuals in my Self-Profile, remain in their Comfort Zones by collecting the information that keeps them at ease. They do this through several techniques that can be summed up as a tendency to *ask others what they are doing*. These traits combine according to the $P = f(H \times E \times C)$ equation discussed in detail in Chapter Two. Because they are information specialists, Comprehenders naturally and automatically use organized, logical thought processes to reach their decisions. They are most comfortable in leadership positions when they can poke and pry until they know enough about people, products, and procedures to make logical, factual choices. They are seldom comfortable with great cognitive leaps which seem to be illogical and careless to them.

It should be obvious to anyone who thinks about the nature of management that such a leadership style can be very valuable to any organization. Few clinics, factories, stores, or hotels can succeed without analytic, logical planning.

Building on Comprehending Strengths

The great strengths of a Factual person include the ability to look at events and relationships in an analytic manner. Comprehenders look beyond surface manifestations to learn enough to lower the risks created by unproven assumptions. By taking time needed to get facts correct and by letting emotional decisions cool during times of conflict and pressure, they can dissect problems effectively and offer more accurate interpretations of what is actually taking place in an organization. It is fortunate that a manager or supervisor in any kind of business or in the professions can benefit by learning to apply the skills that come naturally to men and women with Comprehending patterns.

Unfortunately, using this logical approach, however valuable it is, frequently seems awkward to people on the Compete side of the chart. Managers with Controlling and Entertaining patterns unthinkingly prefer *giving* information rather than asking for it. This was the billion-dollar mistake made by Henry Ford II in selecting only extroverted executives for his company. To him an introspective person was weak and not to be given any authority. And when an outspoken, directive leader dominates a situation as thoroughly as Ford did, it is virtually impossible for an introspective employee to break from his or her own pattern to *tell* what should be known.

Not long ago, an attorney friend of mine with an Entertaining pattern discovered how important it is to *listen* rather than to *tell* all the time. On his afternoon off, Andy hurried into his office to verify one item in a contract, leaving his automobile double-parked on the side street. Once inside, however, he became engrossed in telling a junior attorney how to successfully meet a client's needs. He forgot about his Porsche for 20 minutes or so. Finally, the youngest and newest typist on the staff came into his office and stood shyly by awaiting a pause in the conversation. Andy failed to notice her at first and, when she tried to interrupt, he waved her from the room. He assumed that she had a legal question and said that he would get to her when he was through with the contract.

When she hesitated, he more firmly told her to leave. She did and Andy completed his discussion. When he reached the street, however, after slipping out the side door so she couldn't delay his departure, he discovered that his automobile was missing. Thinking that it had been stolen, he rushed back inside to discover the shy young typist awaiting him. She had been trying to tell Andy that the roaming city tow truck had come and that he should either move his car or give her the keys so she could. When telling about the incident, he had the grace to blame himself and not his employee, though it cost nearly 50 dollars to rescue his proud beauty from police impoundment.

An automatic tendency to issue orders must often be held in check in order to use the strengths of a Comprehender as a means of gathering the information needed to make the best possible decisions. An impulsive tendency to take charge of situations when you have neither the knowledge nor the expertise to make good decisions must be curtailed until you are certain that the right event or relationship has been identified. There is no value in setting out boldly to manufacture buggy whips when one's market analysts know that people are buying steering-wheel covers. As I consult in various organizations, however, I frequently find far greater mistakes than that being made consistently.

The temptation of managers to function exclusively as action-oriented, take-charge people must be tempered by introspectively thinking things through logically before committing time and resources to solving problems. In this way one can avoid senseless mistakes. In their book *The Rational Manager*, Kepner and Tragoe tell of a manager who was faced with an unwanted carbon deposit on the plastic filaments manufactured by his firm. After many trial-and-error corrections which failed to solve the problem, the group finally found a switch engine parking on the rail tracks beneath the air inlet for the building. When the crew walked over to an all night diner for their coffee break, the smoke contaminated the material.

Instead of simply asking the railroad crew to park a hundred feet down the track, however, the manager decided to forestall any possible repetition by fitting an oil bath cleaning process to his collectors. It worked fine, though actually there was no more carbon deposit after the crew parked elsewhere.

Unfortunately, while the oil bath cleaned the filaments, it so coated all the equipment that the workmen could no longer lift the loaded bobbins on schedule. The men were dropping them, straining their backs, and so consistently falling behind schedule that additional men had to be put to work on the task. It was a classic case of fixing something that wasn't broken yet!

The need to logically identify the causes of problems may seem cumbersome to people at the right of the chart, but it would have been extremely valuable to the manager of the filament manufacturing firm in the above story. Problem analysis is crucial because nothing else can successfully narrow a complex collection of raw facts to manageable proportions. A trial-and-error approach is too costly, of course, as well as being too time-consuming. Solving problems by creatively conceptualizing them in a logical manner must be based on facts rather than on intuition or assumptions if you wish to have a high percentage of successes.

Problem Analysis

Each successful manager soon discovers that problem analysis is crucial to effective leadership. In the daily operation of any kind of organization, any well-developed systematic approach is continually complicated by many factors. Internal and external pressures of different proportions and degrees occur from time to time. Because change keeps occurring, there is no way to play an organization's work so well that adjustments are unnecessary.

Problems occur consistently, yet many people in management take them at face value without a logical approach to discovering the actual cases. I have heard some managers say they haven't the time for systematic problem analysis in the daily confusion of getting their work done. Actually, a manager cannot afford to ignore a systematic approach unless he or she is willing to continue working at the lowest levels of management where the problems are so simple that one has experienced them all in the past.

I have found that most managers who resist systematic problem-solving in favor of intuition are close to the edge of the personality chart. They are implying that they are not comfortable being introspective, so they want life to yield its rewards to a simple, directive approach without any great depth of leadership sophistication. Besides, *telling* others allows them to remain in their Comfort Zones.

To use the strengths of a Factual self-image effectively, even when it does not come naturally to you, use a scientific *cause-and-effect* approach to problem analysis. Problems don't arise to complicate your leadership style simply because problems occur. Problems occur because there is some underlying cause to them. Barrels of wine don't collapse *because barrels collapse*, but because they were stacked improperly. There is always a distinction between the cause and the result, and you must find it to discover the cause of any problem.

Just as a scientist collects and analyzes data to eliminate irrelevant facts as a means of identifying the crucial element in a research project, and then tests that most likely factor to verify it, so a manager using Comprehending strengths must deal with problems and their causes. To work well as a problem analyst, you must do three things.

First: You must develop *factual information* since it is

difficult to manage what you cannot measure. You, whether alone or with a group, must collect and organize the facts of any given event into a logical and internally consistent model of the situation. I have found it vital to actually plot the data and relationships on a chalkboard or flip chart to make it more tangible. As a psychologist, I am well aware that managers under pressure, including myself, have a great temptation to engage in self-deception. The human mind has the capacity to twist facts to fit preconceived notions, to meet ego needs, and to get on with the work. By plotting things out visually, it is harder to repress unpleasant data.

You can see this self-centered trait at work in any meeting called to discuss and solve a problem. People from different disciplines or departments toss out favorite ideas until the leader is inundated with irrelevant and often mutually exclusive information. A visual, internally consistent picture is very valuable if you are to rid yourself of complex or confusing information. Without a tangible frame of reference, a manager can soon begin to feel like a ping-pong ball as his people bat him back and forth from one hunch to another.

Second: You must *spell out precisely* the nature of the problem to be solved before seeking the cause. It solves nothing to say that your organization has a *high employee turnover rate*. While factual, such a simple statement doesn't winnow the facts adequately. You don't know *why* the employees are quitting or from which department or division they are leaving. Do they leave your organization because the high cost of gasoline makes driving to your rural location too expensive? Is a supervisor from the old *take numbers and kick arse* school creating most of the terminations? Has another company hired your employees away with better benefits and higher pay? You have a turnover problem, but you cannot solve it until you investigate and identify precisely the cause. For example, not until you know that people are having trouble making ends meet after they pay for the gasoline to drive to work each day, can you solve the turnover problem by renting buses for them. *Third:* You must take time to use a *logical approach* despite the pressures of the moment. Don't spend your time speculating about ideas which do not relate to the actual problem. Your initial logic should use this *Four Whats Exercise.*

1. What is the *precise nature* of the problem?

2. What is the *location* of the problem?

3. What is the *frequency* of the problem?

4. What is the *result* of the problem?

Not only does a manager need information, he or she must know which facts are missing and where to obtain them. It is important to know one's limitations as well as one's strengths. It also helps to be wise enough to recognize which information is crucial as well as which facts are irrelevant to the issue being investigated. A sharp distinction between correlation and causation must be maintained, and that can be done by answering the four key questions asked above.

In most organizations which have been functioning for any length of time, a problem whose cause is unknown is likely to represent a departure from an expected standard. In established clinics, offices, and other organizations, policies and procedures have long been established to guide the group toward its goals. When equipment and people are working smoothly, the expected outcome is almost automatic. It is when something goes wrong in the processes or relationships that the expected results fail to occur and a problem is perceived.

But while virtually all problems are deviations from an expected outcome, not all deviations are problems, of course. A salesperson who exceeds quota, an attorney who wins a hopeless case, a surgeon who pulls through a patient everyone else has given up on, all represent departures from the expected norm, but there are no problems in them. Still, even the massive leadership failure of the English-speaking world can be called a deviation from a long-established standard, a deviation requiring correction!

Many managers and other leaders fail to realize that people work with changing attitudes, values, expectations, and choices today. They do not understand that collectively one's employees are irresistible and that more and more of the work is going to be completed on the group's terms. Leaders who are failing, completely or to some degree, have not returned their organizations to the depth of commitment and cooperation that existed in an era before change became rampant and people assumed power over their own lives.

The standard by which ongoing performance is measured is the *baseline* from which each manager must operate if he or she is to lead in a logical manner. When any activity or product fails to reach the baseline, a deviation has occurred. It is necessary to identify the cause before making an illogical assumption or trying to jury-rig a fix that may or may not succeed.

Problem Analysis Process

If you are in a manufacturing setting, you may want to maintain a baseline of 100 percent of all turret lathe parts being accepted by Quality Control people. This is possible in a zero-defect shop and, with adequate records, any deviation from the performance standard is immediately obvious.

For example, should you learn that an increasing number of parts from the turret lathe section are failing to pass inspection, you know that a problem exists, but you don't know its cause or what to do about it. And you won't know what to do about it until you become a good Factual investigator who handles data well. Use the *Four Whats Exercise* given earlier with the people who can supply answers. Follow this procedure in your investigation.

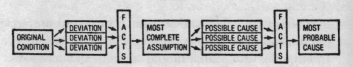

To use this special *Problem Analysis Process*, assume that your turret lathe section begins to deviate from the original condition of 100 percent acceptance. Begin using the process by entering the baseline or original condition in the leftmost box like this:

By collecting facts from Quality control records, you identify the deviations that have occurred. You discover that the brass parts remain at 100 percent acceptance. So do the aluminum products. Only the steel parts have shown a decline in quality. Plot your discovery like this in the process:

The facts of the matter are that only the steel parts are causing the problem. That is plotted like this:

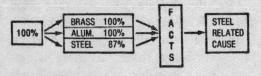

In situations where the problem is human-centered, the facts may not be so immediately obvious, of course. In any case, your search should continue in a methodical manner to identify possible causes. Possible causes could be operator failure, equipment failure, or material failure. Plot it like this:

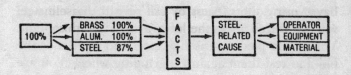

A call to Quality Control confirms that the problem is found only with steel products and reveals the deviations come from all four lathes on both shifts. No one man nor even a single shift is responsible. You know your craftsmen to be proud of their achievements. Several of them have been with you for more than 20 years. They have stock in the company and are financing their children's education with money from the profit-sharing plan. It is inconceivable that the entire group of eight reliable employees has gone bad all at once. It seems far more logical to you that something has slipped with the lathes themselves, so you have Plant Engineering check them out. They find nothing but one warped bed which the operators have rigged back into shape by shimming it with brass plates in a way that none of the maintenance engineers has ever seen before. You make a note to have the craftsmen turn it in as a suggestion, but you realize that machinery is not your problem. Of your possible causes, that leaves only material, the steel which has surfaced several times now in your investigation.

When you seek more facts, you discover that the purchasing department recently changed steel suppliers in order to get a better price. In their contract, the new company agreed to furnish your company with the same quality steel, but you are beginning to have your doubts. Another call reveals that the steel was produced in Japan with a high scrap content. You take a piece of the new steel and a piece of the old and test them against a grinding wheel. You are not certain, but it seems to you that the sparks look somewhat different. You make your decision and order the lathe section to stop turning parts from the new steel. They will have to use warehouse reserves until you can test your most probable cause. The process you are following is now complete.

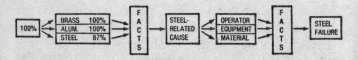

If the laboratory confirms that the new steel does have a higher carbon content and the problem ends when the craftsmen are using reserve supplies, you have found the cause. Have the supplier replace the incorrect material with the steel you need, or return to your old supplier. And have your purchasing manager read the potential problem analysis section at the end of this chapter!

By walking any kind of problem through this analysis process, a manager can identify the most likely cause without resorting to guesswork. It will usually be necessary to seek more facts than one has at hand, but that is what a staff is for. The process is just as effective when seeking the causes of an adversary relationship, of conflicts between employees, or even the reasons for employee alienation.

To test your most likely cause, reverse your direction and play the devil's advocate for a moment. Challenge your own assumptions with facts by seeking out exceptions that will ruin your hypothesis. It is much better to discover the exception in advance than to blunder on with a wrong assumption and discover the mistake after much time and money has been wasted to fix something that is not broken.

Charles, the senior physician of a medical clinic, fired and hired seven support staff people in two years. He was convinced that the younger generation of employees was unreliable and dishonest because of the high turnover. It wasn't until his accountant discovered how the office manager was stealing drugs and his money that Charles realized she was a socio-pathic personality of such hostility that she *forced* the young women to rebel. Because the physician did not stop her abuse of them, they assumed he didn't care and gave him no commitment.

He was appalled to discover that replacing each medical technician and getting her work to the group's performance standard cost around $12,000. His inability to ask questions and to find facts in personal relationships in the same ways he seeks facts in diagnostic procedures cost him about $85,000 in two years, plus whatever the office manager stole. Charles was enough of an accepting person to write each of the former employees a letter admitting that the fault had been his and recommending them highly. However, he could have discovered his key problem years earlier by running the facts through my process to identify a possible cause and then testing it for validity.

Potential Problem Analysis

Successful leaders know that they must effectively solve the many problems that arise constantly in all organizations. Even more important, though, is avoiding problems before they develop. One way is to keep procedures from drifting away from a baseline. When starting new activities and relationships for which there is no performance standard, it becomes even more crucial to anticipate problems.

It sometimes seems to me that too many men and women in management positions dislike considering potential problems when initiating new activities. It may be no more than a Controller's or an Entertainer's desire to *tell* rather than to *ask*, but great problems can arise if a manager fails to ask himself and others what could go wrong in a favored plan. Our egos are so self-serving that we can easily overlook any number of potential problems in our favored schemes.

However, regardless of the reasons, people in leadership positions must regularly ask themselves two crucial questions:

What can go wrong in this activity?

And . . .

What will happen should this plan fail?

These simple questions, asked bluntly of your employees or of your peers, can become a valuable factor in making the best possible decisions in difficult circumstances. I realize, in our positive-attitude traditions, that some managers consider such questions a negative lack of faith. According to the engineering reports coming from the Hyatt-Regency disaster in Kansas City, however, they would have been good questions for an engineer with a Comprehending personality pattern to ask. The lives of many people would have been spared. Still, it is hard to persuade many managers to play the devil's advocate with their favored plans and programs.

Before the Second World War, a major American aircraft company designed a revolutionary-appearing fighter craft. It was a sleek-looking machine with the engine placed behind the pilot, driving the propeller through an extension shaft which permitted an automatic cannon to fire through the hub. The aircraft even had broad, automobile-type doors that enabled the pilot to bail out quickly in case of trouble. In retrospect, the doors turned out to be the best feature of the machine.

In combat, the sleek, modernistic aircraft became a death trap for the pilots fated to fly them unless they used the big doors as soon as an enemy machine got behind them. The aircraft was a failure because executives in the manufacturing firm evidently did not ask themselves several key questions when they finalized the design. They designed the Aircobra with a thick, broad, low aspect-ratio wing that, for all practical purposes, left the aircraft continually struggling to get out of its own turbulence. Evidently, no one asked what would happen if the fighter of which they were so proud were faced by enemy aircraft that used slender, high aspect-ratio wings.

War occurred, the Japanese designers developed a high aspect-ratio fighter—the Zero—and the Aircobra was feared and detested by the men who had to fly it. It could not turn well and could not fight over 12,000–15,000 feet. Enemy pilots soon learned to exploit the superior performance of their machines, and the American government sold as many P–39s to the Russians as they would accept for ground support work.

Of course, potential problem analysis should follow a logical procedure, rather than be conducted at random. Make a chart of the following and refer to it when starting new activities.

WHAT CAN FAIL:
　When new ideas are implemented?
　When time is pressing close?
　When a certain part or process is crucial?
　When complex effort must be coordinated?
　When someone else manages a vital activity?
　When supervisors alienate the employees?

HOW WILL I RECOGNIZE A POTENTIAL PROBLEM:
　Through the knowledge I now have?
　Through knowledge I must yet obtain?
　In new situations where I am uncertain?

HOW SHALL I DEAL WITH POTENTIAL PROBLEMS:
　Which are incidental to my goals?
　Which are important to my goals?
　Which are critical to my goals?

WHAT ARE MY PROBABILITIES:
 That a serious problem will arise?
 That a critical problem will arise?

WHAT COULD BE THE CAUSE OF:
 A serious problem?
 A critical problem?

WHAT CAN I DO TO ELIMINATE:
 The causes of my serious problems?
 The causes of my critical problems?

You can use a simple chart to visualize the potential problems that could arise in hiring a dental hygienist for a medium-size clinic.

POTENTIAL PROBLEM Failure of New Employee To Perform Well		
Probable Cause	Decisions	
	Anticipatory	Corrective
1. Can't do her job.	Verify refs or grades. Give a trial period.	Train to work better. Find a job can do well.
2. Can't relate to staff.	Investigate background.	Train inter-personally.
3. Doesn't remain long.	Verify work record. Use profit sharing.	Increase pay.

A manager who uses this logical approach to identifying potential problems and identifying various causes must draw from personal experience, from recommendations by trusted people, from research, and from the organization's expectations. In a complex situation, the chart may be several pages long. That would be the case in opening a new office, in staffing from a new beginning, or when making a major product-line decision, but the effort is well worth it.

By gathering and analyzing information, a leader can use the searching and discovering skills that are necessary to start a total management approach which transcends any one person's natural abilities. Even when some of the skills do not come as naturally as they do to men and women with the Factual style, anyone can learn to manage the facts that will keep management activities focused correctly.

4

Managing Objectively
(Decision Making)

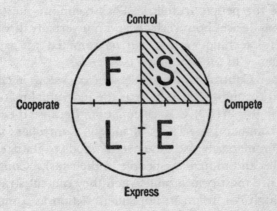

Men and women who combine traits of interpersonal competition and self-control, who see themselves as Self-Reliant, fit in the upper-right sector of the personality pattern distribution. They are the action-oriented command specialists of life who often appear cool in their relationships, precise in their use of time, but more willing to take interpersonal risks than the people to the left of them in the chart with whom they share the need for facts and control. They want figures and data with which to make fast decisions from their more extroverted approach to life and management. Controllers, like Comprehenders, feel all the emotions that people in the bottom half of the distribution feel, but they have a strong tendency to conceal their emotions.

These task-oriented, emotionally self-controlled people, called Self-Reliants in my Self-Profile, remain in their Comfort Zones by issuing and instructions for people to follow. They communicate their strong desires both verbally and nonverbally through several techniques that can be summed up as the tendency to *tell other people what to do*.

Each Controlling person's pattern develops in childhood through socialization as the individual matures in my $P = f(H \times E \times C)$ equation. Because they are the command specialists of society, Controllers tend to automatically use directive methods to initiate activities and to manage people in their tasks. Controllers are most comfortable when they can cut straight through confusion to implement action as a means of getting important jobs done in the shortest amount of time. They tend to be uncomfortable with small talk and introspective discussions.

Such managers have a great deal to offer any kind of organization. Few hotels, stores, factories, or restaurants can succeed without decisive, action-oriented management. Bold, forthright Controlling skills can be a great asset to any group of men and women.

Building on Controlling Strengths

The basic strength of a Self-Reliant-style manager includes the ability to control events and relationships in a positive, direct manner. Controllers want to move out on schedule even if doing so requires taking risks that trouble people to the left of the chart. Such strengths would benefit any person in either a professional field or a business. Any man or woman who learns to apply the strengths and skills that come naturally to a Controller will be a better rounded leader.

Unfortunately, using the objective approach, regardless of how valuable, often seems as awkward to people with a tendency to be introspective, as being introspective appears to a Controller. People with Comprehending and Supporting patterns may even see the extreme Controlling approach as ruthless and bullying. They can, nevertheless, profit by taking some suggestions from a Controller's notebook.

Some years ago, a good friend of mine proposed that we form a publishing company in partnership. We both raised a sum of money and decided he would organize the business while I remained a silent partner. It was a disaster that cost us both a considerable amount of grief as well as money. For our first catalogue, Robert contracted several authors for their next books. Then he rented a lovely office with far too much warehouse space for our initial titles. Next, he agonized over furniture, employees, and even the number of telephones to have installed. With his Comprehending mind-set, he simply couldn't seem to get beyond the details of organizing activities and start the business moving. The pressures increased on him, and, rather than going ahead as a Controller would have done, he kept collecting more and more information. Finally, the authors began withdrawing their manuscripts and the venture collapsed because Robert could not move out of his outer-limit Comprehending style. Today, Robert works as an editor of complex books for a major publisher. His work and his expectations for his job are such that he can remain deeply introspective, but he remains reluctant to make rough-and-ready decisions as is often required in the world of work. Twice in the last six months he has called, asking whether I would be willing to author a book for his company. Both times I agreed and rearranged my schedule to begin research, only to have my friend call in a few weeks to tell how he was having second thoughts about the topic.

Robert remains in his Comfort Zone by asking for more and more information, thus distressing his Controlling boss and his Entertaining author (me) who want to take good ideas and turn them into commercial products in a reasonable amount of time rather than lingering for months and years over a rather simple decision. Unless my friend learns to use some action-oriented skills rather than automatically reacting as he learned to do during childhood, I suspect he will have peaked in his career and never be promoted further in his company.

An automatic tendency to ask for more details must be balanced by a determination to venture forth as a Controller does in order to better direct the activities of your employees. A regressive tendency to wait for more facts can soon reach a point of diminishing returns. There is no lasting value in qualifying and quantifying everything so thoroughly that the tides of time and the marketplace change and your group misses the boat by producing the finest buggy whips in the world. When the time has passed for an activity, lingering on it is pointless.

If you are a Supporter or a Comprehender in the left half of the chart, cultivate the tendency to be more dogmatic when making decisions. Take risks when the rewards are commensurate with acting swiftly and challenging your people to do their best. Use good data, of course, but let people know what you want from them, where they stand, and how you can be satisfied. Once you have analyzed a problem to discover its cause, move boldly as an outspoken Controller usually does to select and solve problems that appear.

Decision Making

Shortly after a successful manager discovers that problem analysis is crucial to good leadership, he or she also soon learns that success comes from making the best possible decision in each given situation. The decisions may often be compromises between the manager's goals and those of the employees, who are working from different agendas, of course. Thus, adjustments must be made as people are persuaded to achieve consistently because of the manager's knowledge of personality and motivation. I will return to that concept in a later chapter, but successful leadership goes beyond problem analysis and decision making in a logical, objective manner to work with people who always remain emotional beings.

Using a Controller's strengths to manage objectively is much more than following a fixed set of rules and procedures. It is also more than reducing each element of productivity to a numerical value and then calculating a score. The people we must blend into a community of achievers are much more complicated than that.

During the years that the United States government was digging the nation deeper and deeper into the Indochina war, Secretary of Defense Robert McNamara was a genius with facts and figures. As a man with a Controlling pattern, he always had a chart which purported to prove that the Communists were losing the struggle. No one could argue with him as he set the stage for an entire generation to rebel in the streets, for ruinous inflation that required a depression to slow, and for the destruction of two presidencies. Beyond the walls of the Defense Department, however, his objective figures were meaningless. It made no difference if he could field 10 South Vietnamese soldiers for every one the North Vietnamese put under arms if the one was willing to stand and fight and the 10 were not. The less tangible trust and commitment of the rank and file made the difference.

Managing objectively remains as much of an art as it is a science. Nevertheless, a Controller's strengths are such that they can be harnessed to advantage in any kind of organization. Managing tasks objectively according to specific objectives enables a leader to communicate what is expected and to receive appropriate information in return. A great deal of guesswork can be eliminated when evaluating both group and individual effectiveness. Rewards can be allocated to the deserving people, and the promise of positive reinforcement can be used to win the cooperation of others.

Leading objectively also enables a manager to make the best choice from among several. Each employee's achievements, potential for promotion, and rate of personal growth can be more easily measured and related to the manager's decision. Best of all, by managing objectively, a perceptive leader can see where to best invest time and resources to gain the greatest ultimate return. A great deal of guesswork is eliminated by working from sound objectives. It isn't accidental that our Japanese and Chinese competitors establish objectives incessantly in their work teams. Both the leaders and the employees know where the group is, where it needs to go, how objectives can be reached, and whether they are being reached.

Much of any leader's work revolves around maintaining the *status quo* of a smoothly operating group and resolving problems that disturb the teamwork.

However, simply clinging blindly to the past, building better wagon wheels for example, is a fast trip to oblivion. Because of this, most managers become involved in developing new products, better procedures, and in setting new objectives for the group. Those who do not deal with new concepts successfully will probably find their careers at a plateau.

As I wrote in the previous chapter, objective problem solving and decision making may be used to return some function to a performance baseline. Even more important, however, is the use of objective decision making to initiate new activities and relationships. Good decisions—those which usually enable an organization to reach its objectives—must be carefully weighed and drawn together. And the more complex an organization and the less obvious a decision, the more difficult a sound choice becomes.

Effective decisions require a synthesis of past experience, sound facts, refined judgment, and an enlightened self-interest. An objective approach to decision making is similar in many ways to a logical approach to problem solving. They are equally important. In other words, the skills and strengths of a Comprehender must be followed by the strengths of a Controller in an analytic task orientation. Objective decision making occurs at three levels. They are:

HOLDING DECISIONS
MITIGATING DECISIONS
CORRECTIVE DECISIONS

Holding decisions are usually of an emergency nature, made at a moment of stress, to cope with totally unexpected deviation from an established baseline. They are generally used to forestall disaster until the manager and crew can repair the hole in the hull of the ship of enterprise. It doesn't really matter who is at fault, why the ship was off course, or how large the tear below the waterline. Something must be done immediately. A holding decision can be of good quality, but it is virtually always used to give a manager time to discover a better solution at a later time.

If a hotel manager finds his basement ballroom flooding rapidly after midnight, the employees and even their families may be called out to protect the property with a dike of sandbags along a rampaging creek. The people, under the manager's direction, are trying to buy time in order to make a better decision in the morning when more facts have been gathered.

Mitigating decisions are usually made to lessen the effect of a problem or a potential problem after the cause has been identified. Often, mitigating decisions are used because of circumstances that no one can do anything about. If, in the case of the flooding ballroom, the manager learns that the nearby creek is flooded because of rain in the mountains, there is little he can do about nature. However, the manager *can* rent trucks and hire workmen to move water-sensitive equipment to a safe location.

The mitigating decision may save his equipment, but it does nothing to return the hotel to normal productivity. Something more is needed for that.

Corrective decisions go to the root of a problem that has been accurately identified in such a way that performance does not deteriorate again once the baseline has been regained. Our waterlogged hotel manager must await nature's shift of moods, obviously, but when the creek subsides a corrective decision can be made.

A survey of past weather reports may show that the creek floods about once every 50 years. In that case, the manager may decide to gamble with nature and do nothing of a corrective nature. On the other hand, he may discover that recent logging in the mountains has denuded the watershed above the creek. With no growth to slow up the flow, the creek can be expected to flood every time a heavier-than-average rain occurs. Clearly, in that case, an important decision must be made.

In the second case, the manager has several alternatives open. It might be possible to persuade government officials to build a dam upstream to create a small lake that holds the runoff safely. The lake could even become valuable to hotel guests who are vacationing in the community. A reforestation project could be undertaken by the Chamber of Commerce. Finally, the manager might decide to have a diversion dike built along the hotel property line to guarantee that flooding shall never bother him again. In any of these three choices, however, the manager has gone to the heart of the matter with a corrective decision.

It frequently happens that men and women in management roles mistake holding or mitigating decisions for corrective decisions because the disaster has been postponed. That usually causes greater problems later since the time available to correct the problem has been squandered for no good reason. The ultimate damage is made worse because the organization's people may accept the lash-up decision as a normal part of the operation and stop looking for better ways to correct a situation.

This happened across much of the American automobile industry when several of the corporations built smaller cars like the Pinto and the Chevette. They were small but still in the old style, with the engine at one end and the drive wheels at the other. A corrective decision was thought to have been made when it was only a holding choice. The lead time was squandered and the survival of several American motor car companies is still in doubt. Apparently no one asked what would happen to the industry should the customers not accept second-rate automobiles when much better vehicles were available at the same cost from other sources.

Decision-Making Process

Assume that you are the senior physician in a clinic that uses the services of four other doctors and 20 or more paraprofessionals. When you visit the Oregon clinic of an old classmate of yours, you are impressed by the orderly, quiet flow of patients which is in considerable contrast to the confusion and complaining that seems constant at home. You are surprised, when playing bridge with your friends, to discover that your colleague's clinic has a greater patient load than your own. You vow, when you return home, to develop a more comfortable method of caring for patients, but you don't know how to start.

To use the decision-making process, follow the flow as you did with the problem-analysis process in the previous chapter. The decision-making flow looks like this:

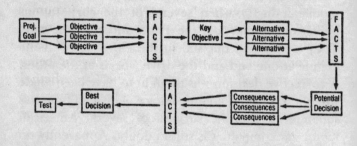

As you did before, place your projected goal in the box at the far left.

Because you realize that each person in your organization knows his or her job better than you possibly could, and because you sincerely value participation and cooperation, you call a staff meeting to gather appropriate decision-making information. You use a Comprehender's skills to learn what people will tell when the boss wants them to contribute. In the honest, unthreatening give-and-take dialogue that follows, some precise objectives arise. The two receptionists who share duties want patients moved more smoothly through the waiting rooms rather than having them backed up because the physicians and paraprofessionals are running over their allotted time. The receptionists feel that the delays not only complicate their work, but also create resentment and frustration among the anxious patients.

Two of the younger physicians immediately counter that by saying they feel too rushed to really relate to patients and to discover the anxieties and fears that come out only when patients are not being hurried through. It takes time to discover whether an elderly patient is actually ill or whether the problem is deep loneliness. They want more time with patients.

Two or three of the married nurses report that they are having trouble with their children's schools. Too often, the nurses must work later than their normal hours while their children hang around the principal's office. An emergency is one thing, but having to call the school office three or four times a week is too much.

By placing the complaints on a flip chart, you reach several objectives which look like this:

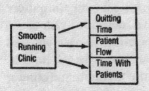

The facts that emerge convince you that virtually every group in the clinic feels pressed for time in some way. In fact, the pressure on you is what made you aware of your friend's smooth operation in Oregon. These are the facts by which you distill the individual objectives.

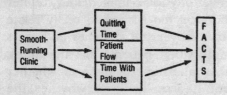

Further dicussion reveals that the key objective emerging from the group to form your picture is the need for more time to work well at the various jobs. You plot in the key objective like this:

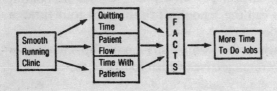

A little more reflection convinces you that there are three acceptable alternative methods available to you in reaching your projected goal, which is a smooth-running clinic. You can keep the office open longer hours and schedule the patients at greater intervals. You can reduce the patient load. Or you can increase the size of the staff. Plot the alternative methods of reaching your key objective and consider the facts:

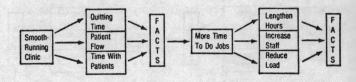

As you and the staff members examine the alternatives, several important facts become clear. The married women in your group, especially those having to pick up their children after school, feel that longer hours would create greater problems for them with their families. A split shift would be possible, but that would entail greater complication in patient scheduling and possibly result in longer delays in the waiting room. Reducing the patient load doesn't really appeal to anyone since the clinic is in a stable community with patients you all have known for years. Many of you attend the same churches with your patients, your children go to school together, and some belong to the same clubs. You have been helping many of them since you started practice 30 years earlier, and you simply could not refuse to see your old friends.

The only alternative that makes any sense is adding to the staff. The patients could be scheduled better, especially with the help of a small computer, and it would be possible for the married women to be finished in time to take care of their families. You consider the possible consequences of your potential decision as the chart continues:

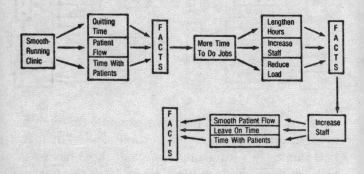

The only question that really concerns you now is the staff members. When you call your practice management consultant, however, his research reveals that it costs you between $12,000–$15,000 to replace an employee who leaves and to get a replacement up to working speed. You are keenly aware that you have already lost one nurse, a technician, and an office manager because of the confused, stressful atmosphere. The situation has already cost you $40,000 and, should one of your young physicians leave, it would double that amount to replace him. In the balance, the cost of another physician and a nurse doesn't seem that bad, particularly if it will take some of the stress from you and the others. These are the personal facts by which you must measure the consequences, but they work out and you agree to increase the staff size.

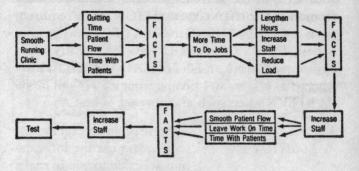

You should follow up to discover whether your major decision does indeed do what you expect of it. You may also need to modify some office procedures and practices to make better use of the people you add to the organization. Any manager must pause long enough to run relevant data through the decision-making process rather than leaping to conclusions without being objective about them.

The Decision Pathway

Since this chapter concludes the task-oriented approach used by people at the top of the chart and the following two chapters deal with the people-oriented approach used by people at the bottom of the chart, it is time to consider decision making from all four personality patterns.

This unique Decision Pathway focuses on the tendency to make decisions from the four personality patterns. As you read and study the remainder of this chapter, look at the way your decisions can be made through each pattern by deliberately shifting your style in the search for better solutions. Work from an EMERGENCY POSITION when required, from a COMPREHENDING PATTERN when that is best, from a CONTROLLING PATTERN when appropriate, from an ENTERTAINING PATTERN when that is best, and finally, from a SUPPORTING PATTERN when such an approach is best.

1. *EMERGENCY POSITION*	Because of an emergency situation, you use the information available to you to make the best decision possible under the circumstances.
2. *CONTROLLING PATTERN*	(Tells others what to do.) You collect necessary information from various sources including your subordinates. You see their task as providing you with relevant information, so you don't ask them for suggested solutions. When you are satisfied that you have sufficient data, you choose your solution to the problem and announce your decision.
3. *COMPREHENDING PATTERN*	(Asks others what they are doing.) You have your subordinates individually give their ideas and facts about the problem. After hearing the appropriate people, you choose

a decision that may or may not reflect their ideas about the matter. You usually keep a complete file of the suggestions given you.

4. *ENTERTAINING PATTERN*

(Tells others what he or she is feeling.) You meet with your subordinates as a group, present the problem to them, and collectively discuss their ideas and suggestions. You let them speak out but forcefully state your own views while urging them to speak freely and decisively. You usually tell why the choice was made.

5. *SUPPORTING PATTERN*

(Asks others what they are feeling.) You gather your subordinates to collectively discuss the problem, its causes, and implications for the group as well as their ideas about a solution. You function more as chairman than as boss without trying to dominate or steer the decision-making process. Because you trust them, you feel you can accept any decision your group makes. Consensus is important to you.

As you work on the vignettes given later, you will see that there is a time and place for each of the five styles. Here are some rules to follow in reaching decisions, however.

Emergency Principle: If a quality decision is crucial and a leader hasn't enough information to solve the problem correctly, approach #1 must be postponed until more information has been gathered.

Compatibility Principle: If a decision is crucial but one's subordinates are not agreeable, #5 is eliminated since they can block implementation.

Unstructured Problem Principle: If a leader does not know where to find needed information to solve a crucial problem, the problem-solving method must supply necessary information. In that case, #2 is out.

Acceptance Principle: When a leader's decision must be accepted by subordinates for implementation and an authoritarian decision does not assure acceptance, #1 and #2 are automatically eliminated.

Challenge Principle: When an authoritarian choice may be challenged by the subordinates who must implement it, because they feel it inappropriate, #1, #2, and #3 are all eliminated from consideration.

Equity Principle: When acceptance of a decision by subordinates is crucial to success, #5 must be used regardless of the time required to get everyone on board with the decision.

Managing Objectively (Decision Making)

DECISION PATHWAY

From the Model developed by V.H. Vroom and A. Jago
in *Decision Sciences*—1974

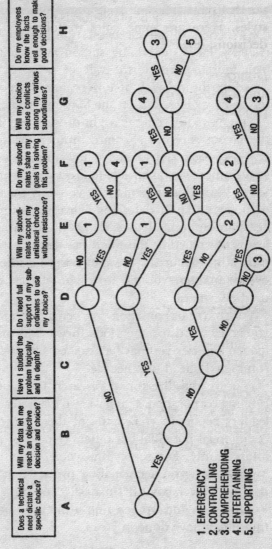

A	B	C	D	E	F	G	H
Does a technical need dictate a specific choice?	Will my data let me reach an objective decision and choice?	Have I studied the problem logically and in depth?	Do I need full support of my subordinates to use my choice?	Will my subordinates accept my unilateral choice without resistance?	Do my subordinates goals share my goals in solving this problem?	Will my choice cause conflicts among my various subordinates?	Do my employees know the facts well enough to make good decisions?

1. EMERGENCY
2. CONTROLLING
3. COMPREHENDING
4. ENTERTAINING
5. SUPPORTING

Vignettes

• You hold the job of general manager for the construction of an electrical transmission line between a large generating station and a major city. You must determine the rate of progress so as to schedule the delivery of towers and other materials to the many locations on the 200-mile routes.

You have driven the right-of-way and surveyed the layout carefully. From computer printouts and past experience, you know how rapidly your construction crews will be able to erect towers and string lines. With this information, you can calculate the earliest and latest dates for delivering supplies and erection equipment to each key location along the line. Your schedule must be accurate since, by underestimating materials, the crews will be idle and, by overestimating, you tie up material that could be used elsewhere.

You have a reputation for being successful, and your crews and foremen look forward to the performance bonuses you have all earned for past projects completed ahead of schedule.

• You are the director of research for a petroleum refining corporation. You have two major teams whose leaders report to you. Some of their projects show commercial potential but others remain of academic interest only. For some time your better team has been working on a fascinating project that you suspect will never pay off financially for the company. Yet the men and women find it the most interesting thing they have done in years.

In a recent meeting with the managers of several operating divisions, a new project with very good commercial prospects was suggested for your group by a manager whose instincts you have learned to appreciate. You see the potential and realize it would be ideal for your top team because of its nature. You also realize that the new project would be far less challenging to team members than the current research.

The team members work very well together, socializing with their families and supporting one another while being very productive for the corporation. You know they will resent shutting their books on current research and that the Saudis would hire any member or the entire team on a moment's notice. The team simply isn't large enough to conduct both projects, but forcing the new research on them would damage morale and lower future productivity, if you could even keep them working for you. The members are so united that by satisfying one member, you will probably satisfy the entire team. You have two weeks to make up your mind.

• You are the sales manager of a small but profitable book publishing firm. You have 10 salespeople who travel in 10 districts in the eastern part of the country. They have come along nicely despite being young, inexperienced, and new to the publishing business. You have personally recruited and trained all of them to the point where they are earning professional salaries and excellent bonuses each year.

Recently, your boss said that the plans you and he have been working on to open the western half of the country have been approved by his boss. This means that five members of your group must train their replacements, move their families west, and accept a reduction in bonuses for several years until the new regions are strong enough to pay off well. In the past, you had funds to ease such transfers, but the recent purchase of the company by a conglomerate ended that policy. They will have to bite the bullet for several years.

Your salespeople are well enough balanced that there is no particular reason to select any given five from the group. Your choice is complicated by the fact that your 10 salespeople wanted a different approach to expansion than the one your boss insisted upon.

• You are the state police commander in charge of a search operation with several hundred law officers, firemen, and civilian volunteers. For 24 hours, the group has been searching for an Air Force pilot who ejected from his crippled fighter above some very rugged mountains. The crew of a passing airliner saw the chute briefly but lost sight of it before they could circle and follow it down. Since a powerful storm center with subzero winds and heavy snow is forecast for the next two days, you must decide whether to continue the search and risk the loss of some lives. However, calling off the search will certainly doom the pilot.

Your search group leaders are all experienced, but with so many volunteers of different skills, you know the leaders will be divided about your decision. Some of them have told you so already, but the decision is really yours.

• You are the office manager of a middle-sized dental clinic. You have recently installed a new data-processing system and instituted a performance team program for the group to use. To everyone's disappointment, there has been no corresponding reduction of mistakes about patient appointments and no increase in productivity. In fact, monthly production has been down for a two-month period, and the hygienists seem unhappy with the new approach to quality. One excellent technician has taken a job across town and criticism is on the increase. A thorough analysis of the software and hardware of the computer reveals nothing wrong there.

You suspect that the new performance team concept is seen by employees as something to trick them into working harder, but the senior dentist and two hygienists disagree. The two younger dentists in the clinic do agree with your view that the quality circles are partially the cause of lower performance, however. Next week you are going to meet with the senior dentist, who is unhappy with the outcome. He expects you to tell him how you plan on reaching the anticipated goals for the new equipment and the new approach to cooperation and commitment. You must decide upon the steps you will take to correct the situation before you meet. Both of you know that the clinic cannot afford many employee turnovers, not with the cost of one replacement running around $12,000.

* * *

As you run these scenarios through the Decision Pathway, follow the instructions given for each personality pattern used. Consider the principles and make a serious attempt to work as a good Controller does when making objective decisions.

5

Managing Inspirationally
(Coaching Employees)

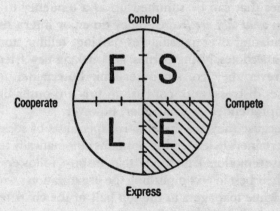

Control

F S

Cooperate

L E

Compete

Express

Men and women who combine traits of competition and self-expression, who see themselves as Enthusiastic from their tendency to direct others and their ability to express themselves freely, fit in the lower right segment of the personality-pattern distribution. They are the outspoken, emotive specialists of society and its organizations. They prefer activities and relationships that are close and warm but on their own terms. They tend to be imprecise in their use of time and are willing to pause in their activities to talk to other people with an enthusiasm that people in the top of the distribution may not understand. Entertainers are willing to accept interpersonal risks as they reveal their emotions openly and freely to people they know.

These people, called Enthusiastics in the *Self-Profile*, remain in their Comfort Zones by speaking whatever is on their minds. They do this through several techniques that can be summed up as a tendency to *tell others what they are feeling.* They do enjoy interacting, speculating over possibilities, talking, telling stories and anecdotes, giving parties, and making new friends wherever they go. An outer-limit Entertainer may cause distress and confusion for an outer-limit Comprehender or Controller, however.

Because they are the emotive specialists of society, Entertainers in leadership positions automatically tend to use emotional methods that inspire followers to do their best in accomplishing the organization's work. For while managers in the top half of the chart tend to focus directly on tasks—with people being seen as adjuncts to the work—leaders with an Entertaining pattern focus on tasks indirectly, usually emphasizing the importance of people to the group. Although both types can do well as leaders or managers, there is a subtle difference. Entertainers are most comfortable when they feel part of an organization in which everyone does the appropriate task in a team effort. They tend to become uncomfortable with too much introspection and delay.

It is obvious to anyone who thinks about work in a modern organization that a manager who can inspire, teach, and reinforce appropriate attitudes and acts by using coaching skills has a great deal to offer. Few private or public organizations can reach their potential with a leader or group of leaders that fail to inspire people to go the second mile willingly and cheerfully. A successful manager is one who goes beyond the use of logical and objective systems and creates a climate of excitement and good will that inspires people to do their best consistently.

Using Entertaining Strengths

One of the great strengths of an Enthusiastic manager is the ability to coach people to give more of themselves in a team effort. By moving quickly with praise or correction and by captivating the imagination of employees with their dreams of success, they work in much the same way as coach George Allen or Hank Stram of the National Football League. Both men admitted freely that their greatest value is and has been in coaching their players to give their best and then urging them on enthusiastically from the sidelines. Allen and Stram were the greatest cheerleaders their players had—and both are Entertaining personalities. Although such enthusiasm may not come naturally to men and women with other personality patterns, every manager can benefit by becoming flexible enough to apply the skills that do come naturally to people with Entertaining patterns.

In the same way as Entertainers and Controllers are not inherently comfortable asking the questions that make Comprehenders and Supporters successful in managing logically or supportively, so people from the other patterns may not be initially at ease discussing their dreams and aspirations openly and freely. But by practicing and performing, anyone can become more at ease discussing his or her feelings with others. Although you may feel foolish leading the cheering section at first, learn some good skills, be emotionally honest with your followers, and give it your best shot. People will appreciate your openness and frankness as you coach them to greater success.

While coaching employees involves techniques of teaching and learning, I am not going to discuss them here. An entire body of knowledge now exists in that area, and any organization's Training or OD group knows it very well. What I am dealing with here are the interpersonal relationships that successful managers utilize as they communicate enthusiasm, use praise, offer emotional rewards, and draw people close to them in a community of achievers. If people need to master pipe fitting, there are many instructors better equipped than I to teach them that craft. What I am doing, however, is dealing with those intangibles that lead to working beyond systems and objectivity.

Communicating Enthusiasm

Through my years of managing and researching, I learned that managers must hold high expectations personally as well as for the group. Communicating enthusiastically is a means of expressing high expectations that, in most cases, lead to greater productivity. Communicating enthusiasm is more complex than it would first seem because effective communication is much more than simply telling men and women what is desired. A great percentage of what we communicate is nonverbal. One study revealed that only 7 percent of our communication is with words. Just over 35 percent is with body language, while 55 percent is communicated through tone of voice.

Virtually every normal person learns nonverbal communication long before speech is mastered. In the womb, a child senses the times when the mother is placid or anxious. While nursing, after birth, each child feels keenly the mother's moods. Only much later in his or her development does each infant begin to understand and communicate with words. Because nonverbal communication is learned at an early age and in a much more intimate fashion, it normally takes precedence over verbal communication.

When communicating in order to coach employees, you must strive to keep both verbal and nonverbal communication congruent. If you make one statement verbally while your body language is saying something else, you confuse and frighten people— especially if you have authority over them. When people are confused or frightened by conflicting messages from the same manager, they tend to work more slowly and carefully to avoid making mistakes. They immediately think that a manager sending contradictory messages is trying to deceive them, or that he or she has lost control of the thought processes. Unfortunately, if the manager interprets the slowdown as a challenge to his authority, the stage is set for trouble that is the manager's own fault.

When communicating enthusiasm, a manager must remain emotionally congruent or *authentic*, as Carl Rogers calls it. In my research and in my own leadership positions, I have found three aspects of emotional honesty that are critical to keeping verbal and nonverbal communication acceptable to your followers. To enthusiastically lead others, you must:

1. Remain emotionally honest.
2. Accept emotions as legitimate.
3. Share your emotions when it is appropriate.

To remain congruent or emotionally honest, a person must recognize what he or she is feeling in a given set of circumstances. A frightened employee who has broken a tool will not believe that it doesn't matter to you if, while you're assuring him, your face is crimson and a vein is throbbing in your neck. The employee sees your conflicting emotions and, because the nonverbal is more important in every person's learning experiences, believes the body language. You would be much better off to speak out as an Entertainer does and say something like this:

Yes, Anthony, I'm *really* ticked off. This is the third straight week someone has ruined a cutter die by working case-hardened steel with it. It does seem dumb to me and makes me mad when my boss reams me for it. I know you are a good worker and a good man. And I know this is your first mistake in years, so forget about it. I don't blame you for the other two, but you can imagine how I feel about the whole thing when facing the Old Man. Let's be careful, *please!*

You have admitted verbally what your nonverbal signs already conveyed, but you have also accepted his apology in a forthright, honest manner that he understands. You have neither frightened nor confused him with conflicting messages. Had you denied your anger, you would have confused him.

The second aspect of remaining authentic or congruent is to accept your emotions, as well as the feelings of others, as completely normal and legitimate. It is normal to feel happiness when something great has been achieved, but it is equally normal to feel anger or disappointment when a great plan collapses. Affection for people who contribute to the group's success is completely normal. So is resentment against anyone who robs the group of its sense of achievement. Fear that follows a close call on the freeway or while installing a heavy piece of machinery is all right. All our emotions are legitimate.

However, it is not always appropriate to express your emotions in such a way that you return to your Comfort Zone. Accept your emotions for what they are—passing, frequently fleeting feelings that can be understood and harnessed without dominating your management style. Once you accept them as normal, you need not deny them to yourself and your followers. Thus you can remain congruent as you talk and as you listen. If you are not an Entertainer, be willing to use your feelings as part of your leadership approach. A great many people will be influenced positively by something that captures their imagination.

Finally, to be congruent, reveal your emotions when it is appropriate to do so. You need not blurt out everything you feel, as borderline Entertainers like comedians Tim Conway or Don Knotts do, but a sharing of your feelings, such as in the example about the broken die, draws more people into your net as good followers. An anticipation of worthwhile activities and shared rewards has an inspiring effect on people who trust and respect you.

Keep in mind that communication includes more than talking or sending memos. It always includes *listening* to the people who work with you. A common mistake made by many managers is to assume that they know more about the job than the person doing it. That is rarely ever true, so give people an opportunity to *sound off to the boss and tell him what he needs to know*. Once you establish authentic communication with people, you will be pleased with what they tell you. They may not always be bearers of good news, but the worse the news, the sooner you need to know it.

Coaching With Correction

I no longer use the words *corrective criticism* when talking about correcting employees. I have come to believe that *all* criticism is taken in a negative way by the people forced to receive it. I have also found that the bulk of criticism is an exercise used by managers to persuade themselves, and their superiors, that someone else is at fault. In any case, it is usually self-defeating, as it creates resentment and resistance among the very people whose good will and commitment are needed.

In too many organizations that pride themselves on their pragmatic toughness, criticism becomes an accusation that tries to wipe out all the manager's frustrations in one great swoop. It frequently begins like this:

Henry, a machinist, has cut too deeply into a part needed for a rush job his supervisor's manager is awaiting.

Supervisor: (Shrilly) For Christ's sake, Henry! You've been here long enough to read a blueprint. Why don't you ask questions if you don't know what you're doing? (You dummy, you.)

Henry: It looked like thirty-thousands on the print.

Supervisor: Thirty-thousands, my ass. You're a goof-off and you always will be. If it wasn't for the union, I'd send you out the gate. But what the hell can I expect from a guy who doesn't contribute to the Community Chest campaign?

Henry: Dammit, Joe, I didn't contribute because my car needed a new transmission. And if you had gotten the print to me yesterday like you promised, I wouldn't have had to rush so much this morning. It's your fault as much as mine!

Supervisor: You hold it right there, Buster! *You* screw up and want to blame *me* for it. You keep flapping your mouth at me and I'll set you down for a week—union or no union.

So Henry thinks about his kids in school, the mortgage payments, and how hard jobs are to find in a recession. He swallows his pride and his angry retort and goes back to work with a burning determination to show his boss that he is not so easily abused. He will take every advantage he can, use every sick day available, and probably vote against ratification of the new contract.

A simple mistake has been transformed into a do-it-yourself tragedy which, if it is a pattern the supervisor uses because the managers do also, is crippling productivity and profits. The employees in a harsh, critical climate must accept management's low view of their worth *or* they must band together in a protective association that gains revenge whenever possible. Most unnecessary conflicts look like this:

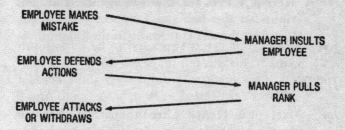

It is seldom helpful to deal with a mistake at the time of its occurrence, especially if the manager is angry. The employee is already unhappy, defensive, and likely unable to hear anything that would be of value for performing better in the future. A verbal attack will only increase the resentment already boiling, often irrationally, beneath the surface. Nothing is ever gained by increasing an employee's frustration, though many managers still confuse criticism with corrective coaching.

The episode with Henry and his supervisor, Joe, did take place. Joe, however, had previously attended my *Capitalizing on Human Motivation* seminar at the University of Alaska. The conversation actually occurred like this as Joe brought the bad part to Henry's bench:

Joe: We have a problem here.

Henry: What's up, Joe?

Joe: It's turned the wrong size. Thirty deep instead of three-thousands. Let's check the print.

Henry: Here it is. Let's see, it was *thirty*-thousands cut, right?

Joe: Right, but it was supposed to be *three*-thousands. Thirty is ten times too deep.

Henry: Let's see.

Joe: Here it is, Henry. Three-thousands—but you have to look closely under the grease smear.

Henry: It's not very clear. It still looks like thirty-thousands to me.

Joe: I can see how it could. But if you had checked the front view, you would have caught the difference. Right?

Henry: Yeah! Gee, I'm sorry, Joe. I should have checked twice. I'll do my best to get it as soon as possible. I guess this puts you on the spot with Engineering?

Joe: Yeah! They'll be critical so give it to me as soon as you can. Okay?

Henry: Right. And, thanks, Joe. I appreciate this.

When Joe and I talked about Henry's mistake, he confessed that he was angry enough to criticize the craftsman rather than correct him. However, Henry is a loyal employee with a good attendance record and high performance, though he sometimes makes careless mistakes. The key to the entire conversation, however, came at the end when *Henry thanked Joe.* Joe had done him no favor except not to make a federal case out of the mistake. Because he coached him rather than criticized him, the craftsman ate his lunch beside his lathe, working through his lunch hour to get his supervisor off the hook with Engineering. When the union steward stopped by to criticize him for working over lunch, Henry ran him off. He was supporting someone he respected and trusted and that was his prerogative.

Rules for Coaching Employees

Managers must keep trivial events and crucial mistakes in perspective when they coach their employees to better performance. A broken hammer is not a broken back. A word dropped in a letter is not a canceled account. And if you want your employees to learn a sense of proportion and perspective, you must lead the way through personal example.

When coaching employees to perform better, there are five rules to follow consistently. They are:

1. Remain as congruent as possible.
2. Avoid bluffs, threats, and psychological games.
3. Emphasize all possible modifiers.
4. Avoid sarcasm and nagging.
5. Lead by your own best example.

Remain authentic: We all have good days and bad, depending on our moods, circumstances, bio-rhythms, and possibly the phases of the moon! These good days and bad do not necessarily have anything to do with your employees' performance. On the other hand, they may have a great deal to do with how people commit themselves in the climate of the group. As much as possible, you should work to keep your verbal and nonverbal sending and receiving free of conflicting elements that confuse and frighten people. Recognize your emotions, accept them as normal, and share them, when appropriate, in such a manner that others better understand you.

Avoid bluffs, threats, and challenges: Any manager's threat, in our era of shared power and incessant change, is only a bluff that has not yet been called collectively by the group. It is often a real temptation—too great for some to ignore. A confrontation is invariably destructive for managers and employees alike, for collectively your group holds your career in its hands. The group can make you look like a genius or like a clod. They can go the second mile because they want to, or they can force you into a heart attack trying to drag them along in your wake. Psychological games are always used to set up someone for pain or devaluation and have no place in a productive office or shop.

Emphasize all possible modifiers: Be very careful of what you promise people who work for you, for you are often the only member of the management team with whom they communicate. Unless you are certain you can keep your promise to people, don't give your word. It is disastrous to raise expectations only to dash them later. Be sure that everyone understands that you don't control home-office decisions, the OPEC cartel, or next summer's weather. By spelling out potential modifiers to your promises, and by keeping your ideas private until they mature, you can avoid a great deal of trouble and remain a better coach.

Avoid sarcasm and nagging: Once an employee has been properly trained, repeating your instructions over and over will only demonstrate your lack of trust or a bad memory. Most employees learn, as do most managers and supervisors, to *tune out* unpleasant static such as nagging, criticism, and sarcasm. Workers do things as they deem best as soon as the boss leaves and care little about the company as a whole. Proper correction should always deal with tasks and how to do them better—never with personalities and motives. A manager should avoid trying to wipe out an entire collection of resentments and frustrations with one swoop. The fact that an employee did not contribute to the Community Chest drive or was late for two consecutive days the previous month has nothing to do with the guidance needed to improve his or her performance on the job.

Be your own best example: The best leaders I have ever known coach their followers by their own examples. History is filled with the names of men and women like Spartacus, Queen Anne, Robert E. Lee, and even General Giap of North Vietnam who took their tatterdemalion followers to heights no one expected of them because they inspired their people. Demonstrating the kinds of values, attitudes, expectations, beliefs, and choices that make an organization great is always the best way to coach.

Before World War II, General George C. Marshall served in many small, grubby posts across the United States and Asia. In most of them the housing was poor, amenities few, and life rude for the soldiers and their families. However, he soon learned how to upgrade the appearance of the buildings after he assumed command of these posts. Rather than issuing orders for a general cleanup, he and Mrs. Marshall would begin working on their own quarters immediately after moving in. In his free time, he would repair and paint the picket fence as she planted flowers and cared for the lawn. She would buy inexpensive cloth and sew curtains while he painted the home and repaired the trim. Later in his life he laughed about it when he told the story. He said that it was a near miracle, for the second in command would appear in *his own* yard the following weekend, and *his* subordinate the weekend after that, until finally even the troopers were working to repair and beautify their barracks. The general said that he never once had to issue orders for the work to be done after he and his wife had set the stage. His followers learned from the example of the commanding officer and followed along. So will yours if you help them feel good about themselves and their work.

The Coaching Process

There will be times when a manager should accomplish something special through coaching. There will also be occasions when employees are so frustrated that they will not be in a mood to listen to you. In such situations, rather than simply offering suggestions, you will need to follow the ASRAC Coaching Process that has been designed to do several things. First of all, it enables the employee to gain catharsis by speaking his mind about the situation. It then enables you to enter into the other person's frame of reference to better understand his motivation. Finally, it enables you to make a recommendation in such a way that the employee is much more likely to agree with it and carry it out. Like everything else in management, the process is not foolproof, but it does tilt the scales in your favor.

Before using the process, heed this warning. There are no techniques which are so clever that they will keep employees from realizing they are being humiliated and devalued by their managers. There is no one method that will not wear too thin to use if it is only a technique to manipulate workers rather than to establish the rapport from which mutually beneficial agreements can be reached. Therefore, use this human-centered process less frequently than the task-centered process taught in the previous two chapters. Don't even think about using this one unless you remain supportive of your employees, or it will create resentment and resistance.

There are five steps to the coaching process:

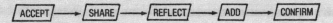

Assume that you are an elementary school principal who supervises a teacher who seems unable to discipline her fifth-grade boys. When parents begin complaining that a few rowdy youngsters are disrupting the others, she either stands the troublemakers in the hall or sends them to you for discipline. Neither of those two options is acceptable to you, for the youngsters standing in the hall are missing their learning experiences while sending them to you makes you the heavy and the teacher learns nothing about how to manage her own class. She is a new teacher, just one year out of the university, but a creative, talented woman who will contribute much to the school once she learns how to organize learning experiences better and to manage a few difficult boys.

You start by calling a conference in which you meet informally in the teacher's room. This is to keep it low-key rather than being called to task by the boss. You, authentically, tell her that you want to put her in better control of her students so that she isn't simply reacting to pressure from a few. You start using the ASRAC Process by asking what she feels about the state of discipline. You ask her to tell you her feelings openly and freely.

ACCEPT

Accept without interruption, defense, or correction everything the young woman tells you, even if

116

she is criticizing you personally and your most sacred traditions. Encourage her to speak freely about the students, their problems, their parents, and anything else she wants to discuss. Listen actively and supportively as she speaks. Maintain a positive nonverbal attitude, letting your body language reflect your acceptance of her as a person even if she says something with which you do not agree. You can even nod from time to time or mutter something like, "I understand," "Tell me more," or, "That's interesting." The purpose of this accepting stage is twofold. It allows her to gain catharsis from a frustrating experience and it gives you information you would never hear should you correct her or dominate the conversation. After all, the entire point of coaching employees is not to prove that you are still the boss but to improve performance. Unfortunately, too many managers have yet to discover this.

When the employee has gained catharsis and stopped speaking, go on to the next step in the coaching process.

| ACCEPT | → | SHARE |

Share the teacher's point of view as best and as authentically as you can. Put yourself in her place with her desire to be successful, her fear of failure in a new job, and all the rest. Share your empathy as honestly as you can by saying something like this:

That must have really frustrated you.
I must admit, had a student done that in my room, I would have wanted to belt him a good one.
I also get frustrated with youngsters who don't seem to care about education for themselves or for others.

When the teacher is really listening to you because of your empathic sharing, go on to step three.

| ACCEPT | → | SHARE | → | REFLECT |

You can best reflect what the teacher is saying by paraphrasing her words and feelings. You can say something like:

Let's see if I understand you correctly. Feel free to correct me if I've missed the point. Okay? Are you telling me that you have problems controlling those boys because their parents let them run wild? Is that what you are telling me?

Of course that is what she is telling you, for you simply paraphrased her words and the feelings gathered from her body language. You, however, come across like an interpersonal genius because no one she knows *ever* uses this method to demonstrate understanding. This demonstration of you as an understanding person is crucial, for psychological research shows that people are much more likely to do what they are asked when they believe their feelings are understood. By paraphrasing the teacher's statements smoothly, you keep her from realizing what you are doing, but you come through as someone who really knows what is happening. This paraphrasing is so important that I will use another example:

> Tell me if I understand you. Are you saying that you love teaching but that the disciplining of those boys is taking too much time from your class work? Is that what you mean?

Obviously, your reflection of her feelings should be done in a supportive manner and not tossed out as a challenge. Only after she agrees that you have stated her position correctly, do you go on to the next step of the process.

| ACCEPT | → | SHARE | → | REFLECT | → | ADD |

Now is your opportunity to add *new* information for her consideration, information that will enable her to resolve her problem about discipline and become the kind of teacher you feel she can become. You think for a moment about several other teachers having discipline problems and the fact that other principals have mentioned having difficulties with their new teachers. Then you can continue:

> I'm glad that we've had the opportunity to talk like this. Research shows that more teachers leave

the profession because of discipline problems than for all other reasons combined. I would not want that to happen to you, for I think you have the makings of a great teacher. So, I have a suggestion. Several other teachers have the same problem here. So do several teachers with Sally Forrester and Pete Kitchen at Ivanhoe and Armstrong schools. Why don't I do this for you? Why don't I call Sally and Pete and draw together a Saturday seminar for a dozen or so teachers? I'll lead it and we'll have several guests from the university as well as some other teachers who have mastered the discipline question without losing their affection for the students. We could do this before Christmas break or right after the first of the year. Which would you prefer?

She will have to invest a Saturday in the seminar but so will you and several other people, so you are obviously being supportive of the teacher. You do want to close the issue with her agreement, however. You go to the final step in the process.

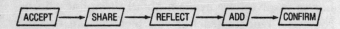

Ask for a commitment to confirm her acceptance.

Which time will be best for you to attend? Shall I arrange the program just before Christmas vacation or just after we return to school in January? Please give me your choice in this matter.

By leading a troubled employee through the coaching process in this manner, you have come to grips with her fears and uncertainties, demonstrated your support and understanding, shown your desire to help, and offered a specific learning experience that she cannot refuse if her career is important to her. You have stacked the cards, in a manner of speaking, but she will benefit as much as the boys and the entire class. You remained the leader but you were supportive and understanding all the way. By demonstrating your concern, you have helped her feel like a full-fledged member of the faculty—a first-class citizen of a community of achievers.

By focusing on human-centered activities like Entertainers do naturally, a manager with any other personality pattern can develop the ability to establish appropriate performance patterns at will by coaching employees better in their times of need. Such an approach may require a few more moments than tossing out a take-it-or-leave-it order, but the results will more than justify the time.

6

Managing Supportively
(Counseling Employees)

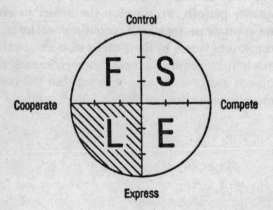

Control

F : S

Cooperate | Compete

L : E

Express

Men and women who combine traits of self-expression and cooperation, who see themselves as Loyals because of their tendency to be concerned with the way people feel and to ask others what they are feeling, fit in the lower-left section of the personality pattern chart. They are the agreement-oriented, consensus-seeking concern specialists who frequently appear warm and supportive of others while in their Comfort Zones. They are often generous with their time and willing to help others understand problems and to seek solutions together in their relationships.

Such men and women relate well to many people in friendship and love. However, they normally do not take interpersonal risks that might damage a friendship unless it is forced upon them. This approach to life and management may cause them pain when they must criticize a friend or an associate, so they sometimes tolerate situations that should be corrected. Of course, when forced from their Comfort Zones by tension that remains unrelieved to become stress, a Supporter can become a fierce attacker who lashes out at the people nearby.

Men and women with Supporting styles remain in their Comfort Zones by working through people in an indirect, accepting manner rather than by focusing directly, on tasks *per se*. Because Loyals are people-centered, they feel that it is only through men and women that worthwhile tasks are completed. Because of this belief about tasks *per se* and the people who do them, they tend to ask others what they are feeling and to encourage peers, employees, and their own managers. They seem to be less aggressive in their relationships than Entertainers, who sometimes seem determined to be friends whether someone else wants them as friends or not. Supporters tend to remain low-key and quietly accepting of people in most situations even when they cannot agree with their decisions and choices. Because of this, it helps to realize that a Supporter may continue to relate warmly to you long after he or she has decided not to do what you want.

Much of the management strength each Supporter uses arises from the belief that an organization must be managed in a way that supports people and does not require people to adjust to the practices and policies of the formal organization. The goals of a Supporter and a Controller, for example, may be similar—*higher productivity and better quality*—but while the Controller almost innately focuses on tasks directly, often forcing people to adapt willy-nilly without regard to feelings and needs, a Supporter takes a different, frequently more effective, tack. He or she is much more likely to see the successful completion of tasks as the logical outcome of cooperative people being committed to one another and to the group's objectives.

Using Supporting Strengths

Anyone who plans to develop a community of achievers from a group of diverse men and women should realize that a manager who supports people emotionally and professionally while they develop their skills will be more successful than one who does not. Fortunately, managers with the other three primary patterns can learn to use the strengths that come naturally to Supporters. Few organizations, regardless of how well they seem to perform on the surface, ever reach their optimal performance without utilizing managers who, through their personal counseling skills, help the members improve their skills and offer more of themselves.

The strength of a Loyal manager, from which each person with another pattern should draw, always includes the ability to guide people toward personal and professional maturity—to counsel them effectively. By planning so employees can grow in ability through supportive attitudes, accepting relationships, and responsible choices, a Supporting manager can work in much the same manner as a psychologist who helps people sift through facts and feelings to understand better the challenges they face and to complete constructive tasks.

One of the things that professional counselors have learned is that people really are infinitely complex. No one, yourself included, has simple emotions or understands them perfectly. We all have motives and personal agendas that remain hidden deeply in the unconscious aspects of the mind to surface and cause conflicts or disappointments from time to time. Many people follow a particular course of action and later wonder why they chose it. In a management position, however, you can hardly be content with imprecise answers from people who report to you. More to the point, you cannot hope to be an effective manager unless you know what you feel and why you do the things you do. The old admonition—*know thyself*—is crucial for managers, for they must remain authentic as they counsel for better employee performance.

The field of professional counseling has long been

divided into two camps. There is the *directive* approach and the *nondirective* approach. But while the philosophers of psychology continue to argue the merits of each, the manager who is on the spot to produce should accept the fact that management counseling requires both methods. In some circumstances, employees need to find direct, *hardware*-oriented answers. In such cases, you draw from your expertise, your library, your computer, and other sources to give the best possible advice.

A few months ago, my son, Howard, who often works with me, developed a plan to market our services to professional men and women in our community. It was a good plan that I was willing to pilot after some marketing research. He then wanted me to decide whether to implement it in Minneapolis or St. Paul initially, since he had no hard facts about either city. We spent some time reviewing his data and then mutually agreed upon Minneapolis for several rather simple reasons. We had better facts about the latter city, we live in Minneapolis so our commuting time would be less, and we simply know more people on this side of the river. I would not have been disturbed had he insisted on St. Paul, but I would have wanted to know his logic before concurring. It was a simple, *directive* decision made by the two of us together.

On the other hand, challenges will arise that focus on emotions, ambition, conflicts, and much more where the best data bank in the world will not help at all. In that case you must abandon a simple, directive approach to counsel in a nondirective manner. Circumstances will determine which approach should be used.

Directive Counseling

The advice or guidance that should be given through directive counseling most frequently relates to the hardware of an organization. For example, when an employee tells you that a marketing program, an assembly process, or a piece of machinery is not performing as expected, a straightforward solution is expected. *Even this, however, is not as simple as it might seem at first glance.* After all, the employee responsible for the work probably knows a great deal more about the procedure or the equipment that you do. If he or she is confused, you are probably in over your head to start with! You may need some sound advice from Plant Engineering or Marketing, or perhaps from the manufacturer of the equipment or a consultant, and you need it as quickly as the problem is serious.

Surely, every manager realizes that he or she need not feel guilty knowing less about a procedure or process than the employee doing the work. In fact, managers had better not know so much trivia or they become lost in detail and not very efficient. I once heard about a vice-president of a large organization who memorized the prices of the sandwiches in the employees' cafeteria just in case the president asked for the information some day!

Such an intensive approach invites your employees

to dump more and more of their decisions on you. I knew one sad middle manager who worked for a *Fortune 500* firm some years ago when I did. I made a practice of not working on Saturday or Sunday, but from time to time something needed my attention so I would come in to the office. Every time I did, I found Roger rooted to his desk, a cold hamburger for his lunch, slaving away while his peers and his own managers were playing golf, sailing with their families, or whatever.

Roger knew they were free while he wasn't, but he didn't seem to connect their freedom to his Controlling need to check and recheck their decisions. He did not realize that his inability to delegate tasks and to trust his people placed the monkey of overwork directly on his back and made him virtually unpromotable. The next manager, to whom Roger was reporting, eventually chose someone more able to counsel employees in new ways to work better together. He could see, as could we all, that Roger's inflexible style made it impossible for him to oversee the work of another level of managers and their people.

Roger could have used the four-step counseling process that is so good when reaching directive, hardware-type decisions. It has the advantage of walking concepts through while helping employees learn how to resolve similar difficulties for themselves in the future. These are the steps:

1. Relating to employees to maintain rapport.
2. Recognizing the situation as they see it.

3. Recommending appropriate corrective action.
4. Recovering opportunities to focus employee growth.

When an employee has a problem of a procedural or technical nature, take time enough to make the seeker feel comfortable with you. *Relate* warmly and supportively long enough to be perceived as an accepting rather than as a rejecting manager. Use the skills that come naturally to a Supporter in this case. Do not empty your basket of frustration on the other person simply because you are distressed. It will surely come home to haunt you later since few people can be abused with impunity in our era of changing employee attitudes.

Because the employee doesn't want to appear stupid or careless, he or she probably would not have bothered you had it not become necessary. The exception to this rule of thumb occurs when a Controlling or an Entertaining manager wants everything under personal control like Roger did. Problems can also occur when a manager of any personality pattern approaches leadership from a *superior* psychological attitude. A manager who conveys the message that he or she sees himself as all right while others are *not* all right will force the employees to check and double-check to keep out of trouble. They keep bringing in lower and lower level decisions for approval so they will not be penalized or devalued.

If you have been trustworthy and supportive of your employees, you can put an end to the adversary relationship that cripples so many organizations by relying on your employees. Assume that they want to achieve and to win satisfaction by working well with you. By *relating* warmly, you keep the employees open and authentic with you and keep them from getting into egocentric predicaments in which they are more concerned with self-protection than in solving problems with you.

Egocentric predicaments occur when people are so intent on doing something well, usually in order to avoid being hurt, that they overlook something equally important. They usually occur at times of confusion and stress, as when a problem needs to be resolved.

Last Saturday, my daughter's car did not start, and she needed a ride downtown to her job some four or five miles from home. Because of previous commitments, none of the family members could offer transportation. She had waited too long to catch a bus, and a taxi, because of costs, was her last resort. She reluctantly called one, but while still on the phone, a neighbor announced that he could give her a ride if she could be ready in a few minutes. Dorothy canceled the taxi and scurried frantically around getting ready. When the neighbor honked, she dashed away to go to work.

She had been gone but five minutes when the door opened and my daughter rushed back into the house to get her materials without which there would be no purpose in going to the job. She was in an egocentric predicament while getting ready and overlooked one vital item. Once on the way, she came out of the predicament, remembered her materials, and returned to get them. Her mind had focused so completely on getting the ride that she blanked out everything else, just as your troubled employee may do unless you *relate* supportively enough to get beyond such a state.

Have the employee become comfortable, offer coffee if appropriate, and talk about something inconsequential like the weather or the prospects of the local ball club. Only after he or she is thinking freely once more should you bring up the facts of the problem.

/RELATE /

To relate warmly, listen without rebuttal, interruption, or criticism. Hear the employee out without trying to fix blame or protect yourself. Let your verbal and nonverbal communication demonstrate your sense of proportion and your willingness to get on with the task rather than making the employee pay emotionally for coming to you.

The next step in a directive counseling process is to *recognize* the situation as the employee sees it. Remember that a desk or bench is the employee's kingdom. Anyone who has spent several months or even years at the job knows it backwards and forwards, so draw from that fund of knowledge for anything the employee may have overlooked in the confusion.

Ask supportive—not critical—questions that identify the crucial facts of the situation. Listen *supportively*, *selectively*, and *rewardingly* until you have the facts you need. Call in technicians if necessary, but continue with feeling-oriented questions as the next step in *recognizing* what the employee knows. Listen for what is not said as well as for what is. Read between the lines and fill in the blanks, verifying facts and feelings with more supportive questions. Always remember that the game is not pinning the tail on the donkey, but counseling the employee to assume more and more responsibility.

When given the opportunity to speak freely, without being blamed or devalued in some way, most employees will reach back into their subconscious knowledge to give the answers you need to direct them more effectively. As an employee comes out of any egocentric predicament, use the Problem Analysis Process and the Potential Problem Analysis Process from Chapter Five. Teach your employee how to use the processes in order to spare you effort in the future. The directive counseling process now looks like this:

```
/ RELATE / ──▶ / RECOGNIZE /
```

After you have come to grips with the situation through your own knowledge, the expertise of the employee, and any technical people called upon, you are in a better position to *recommend* a solution to a straightforward problem. If you have needed advice from someone else, time may have elapsed since your first meeting with the employee. In that case, continue the discussion where it was put on hold as you sought better information. Spend some time *relating* once again, if necessary, to put the employee at ease once more. The process continues:

RELATE	→	RECOGNIZE	→	RECOMMEND

Finally, before applying the solution, have the employee play devil's advocate with your recommendation. Ask for agreement or disagreement and for reasons why. Use the Potential Problem Analysis Process to *recover* an opportunity to use the employee's expertise as a means of maintaining greater participation as well as to keep you from making a mistake. The process then looks like this:

RELATE	→	RECOGNIZE	→	RECOMMEND	→	RECOVER

While using the process, you have remained supportive, have been more interested in getting the situation corrected than finding someone to blame, and have kept the employee involved and participating. Best of all, however, you have taught the employee a better way of resolving problems without bringing them to your attention and requiring your time. You will be a better, more productive manager and the employee a more productive person for your investment in him.

Nondirective Counseling

This second approach to counseling employees goes beyond the hardware of an organization to resolve situations that are more complex because they are located within the software of the group. Unlike the objectives of the directive counseling, which are frequently obvious, the goals of nondirective counseling are harder to identify. This second approach, especially as it deals with individual and group values, attitudes, expectations, beliefs, and choices, must then be more sophisticated than just giving advice, even when you are sure that you have all the information. For example, a manager simply cannot command that two supervisors, who dislike each other greatly, smoothly merge their sections to accomplish tasks which require close coordination and cooperation. The rank-and-file employees will probably have picked up too much nonverbal communication to succeed, and any manager who *tells* the supervisors to do as commanded or hand in their resignations qualifies as dunce of the month!

Much of what each manager learned as a successful engineer, accountant, dentist, physician, chemist, or whatever before becoming responsible for achieving through other people, will be useless or even counterproductive. For example, a physician or a dentist who works alone with a small number of patients can greet each person individually in his or her best bedside manner while escorting the patient to the treatment room. When, however, a professional works with several associates and a dozen assistants in an expanded practice, he or she must rely on a receptionist to care for such relationships.

Most employees who require nondirective counseling need it because they are unable to resolve certain difficulties by themselves. It is usually disastrous for managers, in such cases, to offer glib, simple answers to complex problems. As H.L. Mencken wrote, simple answers to complex problems have a constant appeal, even though they usually turn out to be simple, neat, and wrong.

Even when a manager's answer is correct for a software-type problem, offering a solution does nothing to teach employees to avoid similar situations in the future. A dependency relationship is perpetuated and the organization is crippled to some degree. Actually, most software problems are too complex to be answered by a manager for an employee. For example, what simple and neat answers could you give for the following:

I've worked night and day to prepare for my broker's license and I'm sure I know the material perfectly. But when I take the exam, I freeze up and fail. Tell me, how can I relax so I can get my license and transfer from clerical to the sales department where the real opportunity is?

I know you think I'm the best person for the Omaha office and I would take the transfer in a moment if it was my choice alone. But my husband is halfway through his doctoral program at the university and cannot leave. Is there any way we can work around this without limiting my ambition or my worth to the company?

This company plays politics in making promotions, I'm sure. It's never what you know but who your friends

*are that makes the difference in who gets ahead and
who doesn't. How can an engineer with as many
patents as I have, get past the old-boy network to win
the promotion I deserve?*

Complex problems always require complex solutions if they are to be resolved, and you must not
forget that in working swiftly to get the work done.
Use the Peace Corps philosophy that keeps at least
one eye fixed on the future. If you give a hungry
person a loaf of bread or a dried fish, hunger will
soon return. If, however, you teach the growing of
grain or deep-sea fishing, each person can become
self-sustaining for the rest of his life. Always make
one goal of nondirective employee counseling the
long-term growth of employees toward greater commitment and ability.

It is frequently easier to state what the objectives
of nondirective counseling should not include than
what they should. For example, making an employee
happy or contented is not a legitimate goal of
counseling. According to psychiatrist Victor Frankl,
happiness cannot be seized directly but must be approached in an indirect manner.

In my own *Search For Meaning Seminar*, I teach that
satisfaction is always a by-product of having sound
reasons for life and work to be fulfilling. People, I
write, who worship sincerely, work loyally, love
warmly, and play enthusiastically, seem best able to
find reasons for fulfillment to be a consistent part of
life, whether on the job or away. Nondirective employee counseling should focus on helping employ-

ees organize their work and relationships through the organization rather than at random or, worse, in spite of the group's needs.

On the other hand, making the organization happy with the individual is not a legitimate goal of counseling either. Unfortunately, too many organizations consider a person's ability to placate managers or to get along with peers the best yardstick by which to measure worth and to offer rewards. That is one elemental flaw in the makeup of the quintessential organizational man or management drudge. By confusing compliance with commitment and by seeking personal prestige instead of productivity and profits, many managers want consensus on their own terms rather than on the terms set collectively by the group's members. It is, indeed, unfortunate that many managers still think in terms of the organization being just themselves at a time when group participation is so crucial. Every organization needs men and women who challenge the *status quo* because they think things through at a deeper level than other people.

Some years ago, Walter, the president of a small company, decided that the thing he wanted most in his organization was consensus. Unfortunately, an eccentric engineer who worked for him just didn't fit into any of his preconceived categories. The engineer wore clothes that looked like they had been selected from a succession of dark closets. He would not come to the plant for a fortnight and then come in to work straight through for three or four days on end. He would sleep on his desk and eat fruit from a brown bag he brought with him. He would appear at four o'clock in the afternoon to start working and want a secretary to take dictation for 10 hours. The plant security people complained that at midnight the local police would call, stating they had captured a burglar stealing materials from the warehouse. They would have to go to the county jail to release the mad scientist who was only looking for materials he needed for a project.

It went on like that for a year or more, until Walter became thoroughly disgusted with the engineer. To keep peace with the secretaries, janitors, and guards, he fired the man, who promptly went across the city and went to work for Walter's chief competitor. The president said:

> I surely was smart! I wanted conformity at any price. It was more important to me that no one rock the boat than that he be creative. *I* taught *him* a lesson *he* would never forget. I fired him, forced him to work for my competitor at a nice raise, and watched in considerable anguish as he developed a revolutionary new procedure that gave my competitor an edge which took me 10 years of reduced earnings to make up. I've been looking for another eccentric genius for years, but they are hard to come by. I wish I had been mature enough to keep my ego in check.

Counseling as a Supporter

Nondirective counseling requires a different process from directive counseling, for it deals, usually, with more complex issues. You must always remain as authentic or as congruent as you can, of course, since any difference between verbal and nonverbal messages to an employee will cause two additional problems. When a person receives conflicting messages, he or she automatically assumes that the speaker is trying to deceive *or* is losing control of his emotions. The invariable response to that is to become self-protective in every way possible, including withholding information, distorting the truth, and withdrawing from the situation.

Nondirective counseling should be used in those obscure situations where simple, directive answers, even when they are processed through the *Four R's* taught earlier in this chapter, are not comprehensive enough. After all, in most such situations the person that must ultimately be satisfied is not yourself but your employee. You are seeking commitment and productivity as a by-product of the other person having legitimate reasons to be productive rather than trying to buy his or her time and issuing logical orders. The entire point of this book is that such a simple approach no longer works in an affluent society where everything remains in a state of rapid change.

The ASRAC process, which appeared in detail in an earlier chapter, is also ideal for nondirective counseling of employees. The following is another example for your use:

ACCEPT the employee's statements without rejection. Remain an active listener who really hears what the speaker is saying.

SHARE the employee's ambitions, statements, and concerns by agreeing as much as you can authentically. You can say, "I see what you mean," "If I were in your place I'd probably feel the same," etc.

REFLECT the speaker's feelings to demonstrate your understanding. You can best demonstrate true understanding by paraphrasing the statements after saying something like: "Let's see if I understand what you mean. Is that all right with you?"

ADD new information to help the person seek more information. People need logical reasons to justify their choices which are based on emotions, so give them logical reasons.

CONFIRM the employee's decisions and agreement with you by asking for acceptance. Get the person to commit verbally to close the issue on a positive, easily remembered note.

To help you use the process smoothly, work up a few scenarios and practice them until you know the five steps and can use them without hesitation. In actual use, the process will utilize ACCEPTING, SHARING, and REFLECTING to deal with those emotions that are often confused in making new choices and decisions. These steps allow the employee to return to the specific personality pattern Comfort Zone. Only after he or she is out of an egocentric bind can facts be dealt with effectively in the final two key steps—ADDING and CONFIRMING. This method reverses the usual order most managers use—trying to deal with facts first and only then wondering why emotions keep complicating decisions.

A bandleader, who was responsible for close to 100 high school students and their instruments, used the process after attending one of my Leadership seminars. One of the youngsters missed the bus to the stadium and wanted Carlo to recommend how he could get there in time to play for the game. The boy, speaking in an angry voice, blamed Carlo for his predicament.

| ACCEPT |

Jack: Why did you let the bus leave without me? You said you would put my name on the list at band practice this morning. It really burns me up that I missed the trip because I was busy in shop.

| ACCEPT | ⟶ | SHARE |

Carlo: Boy, oh boy! Did I ever goof. I must have missed you in the confusion. You must be furious. And I admit that I'd be as angry as you, if it had happened to me.

Jack: It's more than the game and the trip. I made plans to meet a girl from Southwest High. She's really nice and she's expecting me. That's worse than anything else.

ACCEPT ⟶ SHARE ⟶ REFLECT

Carlo: (Paraphrase) You had plans for a big date, and I messed them up by forgetting to put your name on the list. That's really bad and I'm sorry for ruining the date and all.

Jack: Yeah!

ACCEPT ⟶ SHARE ⟶ REFLECT ⟶ ADD

Carlo: The driver had a tight schedule, so he left right on the dot, and I overlooked you when some sophomores started quarreling over window seats. But let's try this. Why don't we see if you can get a ride with one of the teachers? Someone usually drives to the game. I'm not going myself, because I have to practice for a concert this afternoon, but someone may.

Jack: You think there's a chance?

ACCEPT ⟶ SHARE ⟶ REFLECT ⟶ ADD ⟶ CONFIRM

Carlo: I don't know, but let's go to the office and find out. I'll do my best to help you find a ride. I can't promise anything but I'll try. Oh, will you forgive me for being careless?

Jack: Uh, oh, yeah! Let's go check. And, I, uh, guess I could have kept a closer watch on the time and swept the shop a little sooner. It's probably my fault as much as yours.

Such a simple process enables you to maintain rapport in situations that have the potential for conflict or misunderstanding when you are refusing to be directive in dealing with another person's problems or needs. You may make a suggestion as Carlo did for Jack, but it isn't your life that must be lived more successfully and with greater satisfaction. The best thing about the ASRAC process when used to counsel nondirectively, is that it forces people to think through their options and to come to grips with their own responsibilities like it did with Jack. At the end, he accepted responsibility for himself and, if he does not find a ride, he will have to learn from his experience.

Directive counseling, with the Four R's, is best used for simple hardware-type problems while software problems should be approached with the nondirective ASRAC process. In both kinds of situations, your goal is to help the employee make the best possible choice. Then it becomes, psychologically, his or her choice and not a solution imposed from without by the boss. There is a great world of difference in the mental set that follows a person's personal acceptance of a solution.

PART THREE

STYLE
AND
SUBSTANCE

7

A Balanced Management Style

Every organization works from its own philosophy of service to clients and customers, although as I stated earlier, many organizations have not spelled out the collective view of management, motivation, and productivity that is so crucial to optimal effectiveness. Too many companies spend so much time fighting brush fires that they neglect building the deliberate philosophical foundation that our competitors have developed.

The time spent developing and disseminating a sound philosophy of service—including a psychologically sound view of management, motivation, and productivity—is time invested well, indeed. For when objective and subjective decisions flow from a cohesive set of ethics, values, expectations, and beliefs about service, they have a much greater potential for being successfully implemented. A sound view of communal service, any size organization, will certainly help improve management at each level of responsibility.

A well-thought-out philosophy of management, motivation, and productivity is especially needed in an organization that is maturing beyond short-term success to long-range satisfaction for managers, employees, shareholders, and customers. In a well-led company, division, or department, where trust, mutual respect, participation in important decisions, and an equitable sharing of rewards comprise the way of life, the members soon learn how to deal with vital issues from a standard frame of reference. Not only do they know how to respond, they can do it without excessive delay, confusion, or conflict. I believe that a professional person, be the individual a manager or an employee, is one who knows the standard responses to problems but who retains the flexibility to deviate when the situation is best served by shifting from the normal response.

Organizational Climate

Every organization has a specific emotional climate that affects, to some degree, everything that is attempted. This group climate can be compared to the physical climate that prevails in each geographical region on the earth. Within each organization, the weather will change from time to time although the climate itself remains constant. In other words, storms may occur for any number of reasons, but if the climate is basically a good one, productivity will continue.

My research convinces me that each organization remains within its climate in order to maximize productivity while working through its people. It is not coincidental that the two kinds of group weather that comprise organizational climates follow the fight-or-flight syndrome that is transformed into competition or cooperation in civilized organizations.

Each organization, like each society, holds certain crucial assumptions about the best way to work toward optimal productivity. Our society and, therefore, most of our organizations think that competition produces the best results. Perhaps this is an outcome of *laissez faire* capitalism or perhaps a result of our preoccupation with sports in which one team wins the World Series or the Super Bowl and all the others are somehow devalued because they are not number one. In any case, most Western managers stress competitiveness to their groups without thinking very deeply about their choices.

In a recent seminar for managers, I had the participants complete the *Self-Profile* that I developed to identify personality patterns. The instrument has a section for use in overall situations such as in the home or with friends, so I instructed the group to use *that* mental set for answering the questions. When the scores were plotted, I found that the group pretty well fit into the four categories.

Then I pulled a switch and had the group complete the matching pairs *as if they were working in their office as a manager*. When we plotted the scores the second time, I found that the majority of the men and women had seen themselves as Controllers. The largest percentage of the group chose the answers that made them look self-controlled and competitive. They did that, I'm certain, because our organizational mind set requires competitiveness of us.

On the other hand, most Asian organizations, particularly the Japanese and Chinese, prefer to cooperate in their business and commercial activities. They research thoroughly, discuss the implications of their findings at every level of the work group, and plan very well together. I find that the Asian people don't "attack" a problem but "dismantle" it in their thoroughness. They compete when it is useful, but their competition rises out of the cooperation that precedes it. I need not spell out the effectiveness of their approach to anyone who has not spent the last 10 years on the dark side of the moon!

My research, both in the English-speaking nations as well as in Asia, convinces me that we need not demand cultural shifts that would be very difficult to obtain, but should build on what already exists. I find that a synthesis of cooperation and competition is best in Western culture. After all, most managers who use competitive instincts know that holding contests, for example, which are won repeatedly by the outstanding salespeople or employees creates a disincentive to everyone else.

By combining the competitiveness of some people and the cooperation of others, managers can accomplish the most for the smallest investment of time and energy. A degree of competition produces task tension—the knowledge that something must be done within a limited amount of time—that sets people to work with renewed enthusiasm. But while moderate amounts of competition create task tension, too much competition produces *conflicts* that reduce the effectiveness of the group. Conflicts of almost any kind lead people to invest too much time and energy in self-protection to the detriment of productivity.

Cooperation leads men and women to develop a sense of community—to become a community of achievers while completing their activities for the company. On the other hand, too much cooperation frequently leads to *complacency* about responsibilities and assignments. Neither *conflict* nor *complacency* produces the kind of climate that is needed to win the greatest degree of productivity for the investment.

The ideal balance between competition and cooperation looks like this:

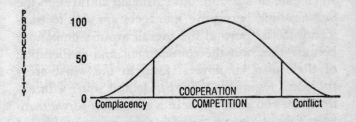

Each organization's climate, which like its philosophy is seldom planned deliberately, reflects past and present management teams' views of competition and cooperation. The executives' personality patterns. attitudes, values, and expectations about cooperation and competition are crucial in the establishment of a balanced climate that uses both emotions contingently.

No one has as much influence on the climate as the chief executive. I have already mentioned how General George C. Marshall led his people in sprucing up their quarters in the years before his rise to power as the U.S. Chief of Staff in World War II. The CEO sets the tone for virtually everything that follows when he has enough tenure to affect major changes in the organization. There is no doubt that such giants as Watson of IBM, McKnight of 3M, and Norris of Control Data set the stage for their followers to achieve a great deal in the years of their leadership.

At each level of an organization, managers and supervisors can balance the use of cooperation and competition to maintain a climate that lessens conflict and complacency. It is true that the practices coming from the executive suite determine the overall climate of a group, but sprinkled all through the organization, perceptive managers are able to transcend, to rise beyond the overall group's limitations because they win the commitment and cooperation of their own employees. Even in the worst army there are regiments that sparkle and shine with enthusiasm and ability. There is no reason why a manager cannot choose to have such a community of achievers to further his or her own career while sharing the rewards with the people who help win the heights.

I recently completed a consulting program for the fire department in a large Western city. The organization's climate does not please the new chief, who is a very competent and ambitious young man. His immediate predecessor worked from too cooperative an orientation that led to complacency, and the man who preceded *him* worked from too competitive a position that led to frequent conflict, so a new balance is being sought by the present CEO.

Some battalion chiefs, who won their gold shields before the present chief took charge, still think in terms of dominating their followers. Others want to avoid as much responsibility as possible. Because of the radical shift from conflict to complacency, the different battalions function more like a loose collection of regiments rather than as a united command. Emotional storms are frequent as some men seek power and privilege without assuming commensuarate responsibility, and other men seek to maintain the casual relationships with the firefighters they started with some 15 or 20 years ago.

Interestingly enough, the department is rated most highly in efficiency, for the conflicts and complacency vanish when they are fighting fires in the city. The entire group snaps to with a vengeance, obeying orders instantly, using the members' initiative to best advantage when the safety of the community is threatened. I predict that the group will come around in time, for the present chief is a strong man who understands the need to balance leadership and administrative skills.

Leadership and Administration

Any serious attempt to create a community of achievers that will push the leader to success in his or her organization must include more than a balanced climate. It must also include a balanced view of management. Herzberg used the illustration of Richard the Lionhearted to demonstrate the need to balance the use of hardware and software in an organization, though Herzberg did not use my terms. He wrote that the Norman king of England was a terrible *administrator* of hardware in his organizations. He so seldom could get the troops and the supply wagons together that his crusaders fought hungry most of the time. On the other hand, Richard was such a charismatic *leader* that he persuaded half the men of military age in England to follow him into battle.

Each manager must deal with drill motors, trucks, forms, silverware, buildings, food, and so on—the *hardware* that has been used to help people move through their missions for the organization's clients. Sometimes the hardware creates a problem for the manager using it.

For example, the fire department I consulted purchased a supply of five-inch synthetic hose that would not rot or mildew and that would pass a large volume of water. No one wanted it but the new chief, who had his way. City officials were unhappy with the change. So were some battalion chiefs and many of the men, for it necessitated new techniques in using and storing the hose. Fortunately, resistance collapsed during the first fire at which the new hose was used. Everyone from deputy chiefs to the newest recruit could see the advantage immediately, so the resistance ended.

Such resistance and resentment to new hardware is not unusual, especially if the employees see it as a loss of opportunity for them to maintain status and self-esteem in the oranization. That resistance, however, is seldom as great as it is when new *software* is introduced—when people are required to change their relationships and behaviors in the group. The fire chief is still struggling to create a new climate within his group, although the hose issue was resolved in a few hours of use on a fire call.

Changes in hardware require insight, planning, and efficient administration of resources to make the best use of the tangible elements of production. Otherwise, damage, waste, duplication of effort, resentment, and obsolescence of equipment can follow, so it is when dealing with a group's hardware that effective *administration* is needed consistently.

On the other hand, few men and women are ever inspired to become a community of achievers because a manager has a good grip on the transportation budget or ships the products to the customers on schedule. The rank-and-file employees who make or break managers' careers with their commitment or lack of it need something more to stir their emotions. They need leaders whom they can trust and respect because they are handling the software wisely.

Men and women are not really automatons to be set working and ignored until they malfunction. Neither are they computers to be programmed and then put to work day after day. People cannot be considered inventory either, to be used without regard for their emotions and needs. Humans are, and shall remain, emotional, sometimes fearful, sometimes brave, *always* creative beings who live in a largely subjective world.

Recent research through the National Judicial College reveals that even eyewitnesses are so biased that it may be a travesty of justice to use them in highly emotional cases. For managers, this implies that people are not "human resources" but beings who need support and challenges if they are to reach their potential. It is the human element that our Asian competitors have utilized so well and that we have frequently ignored in our decision to objectify and systematize our organizations. It is when this subjective human element is blended with the objective hardware of our organizations that optimal success is won. Then productivity becomes the logical by-product of having legitimate reasons to give the employees' best to their managers and to their organizations.

Leadership, as opposed to simple administration, includes the ability to capture the imagination of people, to grip the loyalty of work teams, and to inspire individuals to do more than they deemed possible before meeting the leader. This utilization of people must be consistently innovative, because nothing remains static. Virtually every organization of consequence has seen its people change dramatically in the last few years.

One giant corporation that even controlled the day the managers could change from long-sleeve white shirts to short-sleeve white shirts just a decade ago, found itself with a revolution on its hands recently. The company took a group of some 25 or 30 new managers from all over the United States to a month-long program in San Francisco. They arrived late at night, were checked into a hotel, and were awakened early the next morning for seminars. The classes were terrible: they were lectures that went on and on, with no opportunity for discussion or participation, and lasted for 12 or more hours each day. Then, instead of being topics of interest, the content of the program was company doctrine and serious indoctrination.

After several days of lectures, the group began to rebel. The young men and women pointed out everything that was wrong with the teaching method, the content, and the attempt at brainwashing them to accept company policy as right under all circumstances. One young man took time off to visit an art institute that interested him and returned with the recommendation that the others visit it also.

Within 12 hours, his boss and the vice-president of his division had been called to San Francisco to meet with the young man. Did he, they wanted to know in no uncertain terms, have such irrelevant outside interests as art, music, and theater? If so, it would probably be the end of his career in the corporation. He thought about it for a moment and told them that he did, indeed, have interests besides making money for the company. Furthermore, he brought the matter to the next meeting of the training group and started an *open* rebellion. The entire group demanded to know what was required of them, whether they were expected to sacrifice everything that made them human, whether being businessmen and women meant they could not have love lives, esthetic interests, and normal development as human beings.

The conflict grew so profound that the group was disbanded and returned to their local organizations around the country. Then, within three or four days, the students were smuggled out of their organizations, without their managers knowing where they were going, and flown to the corporate headquarters where they were met by senior vice-presidents who wanted to know what had gone wrong. Why, they asked, did this group rebel against everything that all the previous groups had accepted as reasonable and fair? The top management group seemed as frightened as the Czar's cabinet just before the Russian Revolution, and the young man who wanted to smell the flowers soon left the company. He is, I'm pleased to say, very successful in an organization that understands people as they really are rather than trying to turn them into automatons.

The corporation, I am equally pleased to say, has been rethinking its position, even sending investigators to Japan in an attempt to learn. New leadership has decided in this era of change, that leading people to work smarter rather than forcing them to work so hard and so long that their marriages and family lives collapse is far more productive in the long run.

The greatest single change among managers and employees, my research convinces me, is that many, if not most, people no longer believe that teachers, pastors, politicians, *and* managers know what is best for them. This skepticism can be seen in current consumer and environmental groups, anti- and pro-nuclear protests, political caucus meetings that take candidate selection out of the smoke-filled back room, and much more. In every segment of society across the English-speaking world, men and women are demanding participation in activities that are important to them. Business organizations have just felt the cutting edge of this revolution in cultural expectations as people take more responsibility for what they believe to be in their own best interests.

Because *leadership* deals primarily with people while *administration* deals largely with resources, participative or contingency management can be shown with this equation:

$$\text{PARTICIPATIVE MANAGEMENT} = f\left(\frac{\text{Interpersonal}}{\text{Leadership}} \times \frac{\text{Technical}}{\text{Administration}}\right)$$

Because of my own experiences, I believe that participative management—in which more people of any given organization are drawn more deeply into the manager's net to respond positively to a better understanding of interpersonal relationships, to become first-class citizens in a community of achievers, and to share equitably the rewards of commitment—is really the only way we shall compete with the Asian and European competitors that are placing us under such pressure to perform.

The balance needed to become a successful, participative manager look like this:

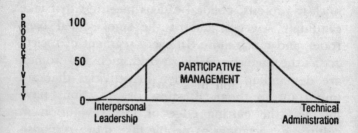

Different men and women, with different personality patterns, attitudes, values, and expectations, working in different settings, will have their personal productivity curves skewed somewhat by circumstances. For example, a youthful infantry platoon lieutenant who leads 36 or so riflemen will need to be more concerned with interpersonal leadership than his Air Force counterpart who flies a fighter aircraft and commands no one. The manager of productivity in an electronics plant will need to be more leadership-oriented than the controller who oversees his finances. All of them, however, will need to strike some kind of balance that is right for their situations, personality patterns, and expectations.

Management Style Assessment

This test instrument was developed for use especially in the DeVille Productivity Improvement System of which this book is also a part. It is intended for the use of managers and supervisors in a wide variety of organizations as they seek for greater productivity and higher quality. The assessment instrument is self-scoring; the interpretation appears at the end of this chapter.

By following the directions, you can gain a better understanding of how well you are balancing the dual factors of interpersonal leadership and technical administration in a participative approach to management.

Using the Instrument

This test or instrument uses your personal views about your relationships with your employees. Therefore, be as perceptive as possible about your attitudes and acts. This is not a test in the conventional sense, for there is no passing or failing. It is an attempt to find where you stand, so that your personal management style can be improved.

Make your selection of word pairs according to the way you normally interact with your employees. Do not consider those times when you are frustrated and out of your Comfort Zone. Neither should you compare the words to the times you are with your family or friends away from work.

STYLE AND SUBSTANCE

1. Choose from the word pairs.

After the sample listing below, you will find three columns of eight words each in a box of three sections. The sets describe certain management traits in two lines.

Carefully read the two pairs of words in each set.

Mark with an **X** the word that *most* accurately describes your attitudes and acts with your employees.

Mark with a ✔ the word that *least* accurately describes your attitudes and acts with your employees.

Complete all 24 sets.

2. Sample Marking.

M O S T	L E A S T		The manager who marked this sample *most* saw himself as cooperative and *least* saw himself as controlled.
⊗	O	COOPERATIVE	
☐	☑	CONTROLLED	

A Balanced Management Style

Complete the 24 sets below.

	M O S T	L E A S T

M O S T	L E A S T		M O S T	L E A S T		M O S T	L E A S T	
O	O	COOPERATIVE	O	O	COMPASSIONATE	O	O	RECEPTIVE
□	□	CONTROLLED	□	□	ORDERLY	□	□	LOGICAL
O	O	EMOTIONAL	O	O	CREATIVE	O	O	PROFICIENT
□	□	OBJECTIVE	□	□	SYSTEMATIC	□	□	FRIENDLY
O	O	IMPERSONAL	O	O	INNOVATIVE	O	O	NEGOTIATING
□	□	RESPONSIVE	□	□	STRICT	□	□	FIRM
O	O	DELIBERATE	O	O	FLAMBOYANT	O	O	ASSERTIVE
□	□	ENCOURAGING	□	□	ADMONISHING	□	□	COMPROMISING
O	O	THOUGHTFUL	O	O	SUBJECTIVE	O	O	CONTENDING
□	□	PLAYFUL	□	□	CONFORMING	□	□	INFLUENCING
O	O	ENTHUSIASTIC	O	O	RATIONAL	O	O	EXPEDIENT
□	□	METICULOUS	□	□	OUTGOING	□	□	ADAPTIVE
O	O	DARING	O	O	ORGANIZED	O	O	INSPIRING
□	□	CORRECT	□	□	STIMULATING	□	□	CONFIDENTIAL
O	O	EXACTING	O	O	TOLERANT	O	O	DIRECTING
□	□	UPLIFTING	□	□	ADHERING	□	□	COLORFUL

3. Scoring Instructions:

Count the *squares* that you marked *most* and place that figure in the ⒜ section of the *most* column of the Computation Grid below.

Count the *circles* that you marked *most* and place that figure in the Ⓛ section of the *most* column in the Computation Grid.

Count the *squares* that you marked *least* and transfer that score to the Ⓐ section of the *least* column in the Computation Grid.

Count the *circles* that you marked *least* and transfer that score to the Ⓛ section of the *least* column in the Computation Grid.

COMPUTATION
GRID

Ⓐ			
Ⓛ			
	MOST	LEAST	BALANCE

To find the *Balance* score, subtract the *least* number from the *most* number for both squares and circles. If the *least* number is greater than the *most* number, enter the difference as a negative number in the *Balance* column (–4, –3, etc.). If the *most* number is greater than the *least* number, enter it as a positive number in the *Balance* column (4, 7, etc.).

4. Plotting the scores.

To plot your score, enter the figure from the *Balance* column on each side of the scale. Enter the Ⓐ figure at the appropriate number on the Ⓐ end and the Ⓛ figure at the appropriate number on the Ⓛ end. This first scale shows your National Management Style, the style you use without thinking about it.

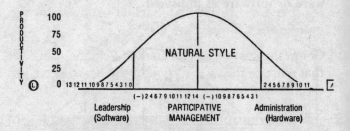

To plot your Idealized Management Style, enter the totals from the Ⓐ and the Ⓛ boxes of the *most* column at the Ⓐ and the Ⓛ ends of the scale below.

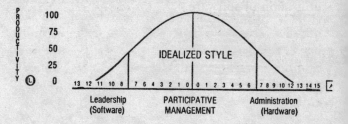

The figure below is a sample to help you mark your own correctly. Assume that you have scored a −11 for your Balanced Ⓛ score and a 9 for your Balanced Ⓐ score. Mark at the appropriate places and connect the figures through the center part of the scale. Your shaded area will reveal any bias that you may have toward too great a concentration on administration or leadership that might lessen your balanced effectiveness. If you find a serious imbalance, work at a better use of hardware or software as indicated.

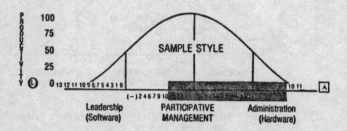

A pattern like the one shown above is skewed in the direction of administration. An individual with this kind of distortion should work at gaining a better balance in the use of hardware and the utilization of software.

8

Building A Community Of Achievers

One recent research study, conducted by industrial psychologists, revealed both good news and bad for managers who want to draw their employees together into strong work teams that accomplish a great deal together. The researcher found that more than 90% of the people sampled want to work at tasks that challenge and stimulate them, at jobs that are worth investing their lives in. They reported that should they win the Irish Sweepstakes, they would continue working for pay outside the home. That is good news—people actually want to work.

The bad news is that most of the men and women said they would quit their present jobs because they were meaningless to them personally. Evidently the majority of supervisors and managers in our society have failed to utilize the widespread desire of people to be needed and to work at purposeful tasks.

I am convinced that the situation will never be corrected until the employees in our organizations discover reasons to commit themselves wholeheartedly to the organization and its leaders. It is obvious that not all jobs can be stimulating or satisfying all the time. Some work will always remain difficult and unpleasant. Yet the development of positive, rewarding relationships will create a community spirit that is as effective in developing an achievement-oriented group as anything else.

When I was younger, I remember seeing the cane-cutting crews up north on Cape York, above Cairns in Queensland, Australia. The men worked half-naked in the tropics, sweating in the heat and fighting the humidity and the insects. Yet there was a competitive camaraderie as they worked very hard to cut more cane than their mates and then worked even harder to surpass the other crews. After a few seasons at Cairns, the other members of the crew meant more to some men than their own families.

My own research confirms that people are motivated to do the things that are important to them personally. In 1981, the United States Department of Labor released a study which revealed that 40 firms sharing a common experience increased their productivity an average of 150%. The companies, ranging in size from a few dozen employees to several thousand workers, were either manufacturing or service organizations.

The 40 firms received no influx of capital, bought

no new equipment, and hired no significant number of new employees in their explosion of productivity. They did not initiate a formal incentive program nor did they create quality circles. The increase in employee productivity occurred because it suddenly became important personally for the employees to work better and more accurately. Why? In each of the 40 companies studied, the employees banded together to jointly *purchase* the organizations from the previous owners! They had become worker/capitalists.

Youngstown Hose in Ohio, with some 1500 employees, had a 68% productivity increase the year following the employees' purchase of the company, accompanied by such an increase in quality that all but 3 of 28 inspectors were returned to productive work. People work hard together when it is in their best interest to do so.

Another study of those 40 firms, conducted at long range by one psychologist who doesn't know a turnbuckle from a drill motor, purported to find no personal involvement by those employees. He reached this conclusion based on the fact that the absentee rate remained unchanged. Unfortunately the researcher, who knew little about productivity and production workers, used too simple a model. He missed the entire point that the massive increase of goods and services created. When a lathe operator or a salesperson has a performance base of 500 units per month, a day off may be a significant loss to the company. When, however, the employee has boosted productivity of 1200 units, with no increase in capital costs, the worker may feel justified in taking an occasional day for personal activities—just as most owners do when they play golf or join in family outings!

If you find shareholders reluctant to give or sell the company to the employees, all is not lost. However, you must do something almost that dramatic in today's adversarial climate. *You must give the company to the employees psychologically and spiritually! You must give the employees the ownership of the company's challenges and rewards so that increased quantity and improved quality will become important to them personally.*

Incentive Programs

Not long ago, I was reading a report in the Alexander Hamilton Institute's *Executive Development Newsletter* in which the author quoted research that purported to show that incentive programs seldom have any long-range results. The author was right—if he was referring to the use of incentives as another panacea with which to correct decades of poor management. When a CEO calls in an ashtray and bookend salesperson to compensate for a horrendous adversary relationship between managers and employees, he is engaging in wishful thinking. The employees will see through the sham instantly, and it may well backfire.

One company I consulted after the fact had a president who seemed to enjoy turmoil and conflict. He had nothing good to say about the workers who were at swords' points with the entire management/supervision group. Someone, however, persuaded the management team to give the employees a token of their esteem. They gave everyone a plastic, ball-point pen with the company logo in genuine gold-colored paint. Regardless of the motives, the workers perceived the gift as an insult, and the pens began surfacing in the most unusual places. They were found rammed into gear boxes, under sprockets, through product packages, and even in the radiator of the president's new Cadillac. Such an incentive program, even had it been followed with other gifts, would not have worked.

On the other hand, a well-planned incentive program can be connected to improved performance in such a way that the return for every dollar invested is from $7 to $55—*off the top*. When an incentive program is like my "White Hats" program or like Bob Schwartz's "Bad Guys" program, it becomes fun and breaks up the routine of ordinary work life. The most spectacular return I've seen came from Silicon Valley, where a computer company employee casually told his supervisor to vacuum the carpet-covered work-benches. They did and recovered almost $100,000 in precious metals that had been going to waste.

When $10,000 is invested for $300,000 return—in off-the-top dollars—an incentive program is well worth the effort. An incentive program, however, can be even more valuable when it is used to create interest in quality circles or performance teams. An incentive program can be part of organized change to create a community of achievers in which the people work well together because it is in their best interest to do so.

As I have said previously, men and women frequently resist change even when it is in their best interest to accept it. Kurt Lewin, the brilliant psychologist who fled Nazi Germany, suggested several ideas about managing change successfully, and my research has taken me beyond that.

Organizations that have a stable emotional climate feel few reasons to change. Collectively, there was no reason for American and British automobile executives to rock the boat with design changes when there was no demand for fuel-efficient vehicles. Yet each management team is challenged by its shareholders and by its employees to peer into the future. When the need to change arises, there is a procedure that can be followed to bring it off with the cooperation and acceptance of the supervisors, managers, and employees. You can win a change in attitudes or behaviors by using the following process:

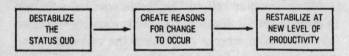

By conducting a fun-filled, exciting incentive program like the "White Hats" program, in which managers, executives, supervisors, and employees take an old-fashioned temperance-type pledge to save the company a dollar a day, wear cowboy boots and hats, and win really valuable prizes like a new pickup truck or a trip for the entire family to an Arizona guest ranch, the routine can certainly be destabilized. An incentive program, to be most effective, must be part of something more sophisticated, however. During the fun, the employees must perceive reasons to change and accept new relationships and activities.

The reasons for change to occur in an organization can come from the concepts taught in this book and in my programs. People need esteem, participation, growth, and satisfaction from working well together with people they respect and trust. They must find reasons through motivation: by *having* desirable things, *doing* interesting activities, and *becoming* first-class citizens of the group. Then, through participation in problem identification and resolution programs (properly called *performance teams* rather than quality circles), the group is restabilized at a new level of productivity and satisfaction.

This approach works very well in those organizations where the managers have made the special effort to establish a new level of trust and mutual respect between themselves and the employees. The incentive program should be deliberately developed to disrupt the routine of work with something exciting and challenging to large numbers of employees. And while I am not completely unbiased, I believe that the "White Hats" program, in its cowboy/western motif, is best suited to do this in most organizations. When that program is followed by the development of performance teams, the progress looks like this:

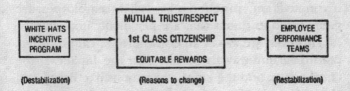

STYLE AND SUBSTANCE

The use of an incentive program that leads into quality circles, or better yet, performance teams, has repeatedly proven so effective that it will consistently lead to the same level of productivity with a 33% reduction in labor costs. The typical manufacturing company that uses one also finds a 25% reduction in required floor space and a 66% reduction in inventory. And while giving the company to the employees physically produces an average increase of 150%, giving it to them psychologically and spiritually produces a 36% to 75% increase with the added advantage that the shareholders still own the company.

According to *Business Week*, any kind of incentive program or performance team approach must be sponsored and steered by the chief officer of a company. I agree, for this is too important to be handled at a lower level. A deputy can and should be assigned the actual task, but the CEO must be visible and involved or the program will limp along badly. Unfortunately, too many CEOs have risen to preeminence because of their financial ability to wheel and deal with bankers, investment specialists, and shareholders. After all, as Deming has said, no president was ever fired because the quality of products was low, but many have lost out because the company stock performed poorly on Wall Street. Going back to motivation, presidents as well as employees are committed to things that are personally important!

However, we are in an era where we cannot wheel and deal our way financially past the Japanese, the Europeans, and the emerging nations like Brazil and possibly India. To compete, we have to produce the goods and services that will attract and keep customers rather than satisfy bankers.

The entire point of an incentive program is to catch the employees doing good things and to reward them for it. After all, each company produces the goods and services that the management team collectively reinforces, though the level of performance is frequently neither what the managers wanted nor expected.

To have a successful incentive program, offer the participants the largest number of best quality rewards you can afford. Connect the giving of the rewards to participation and improved performance, and do this as rapidly and as dramatically as possible. Use the community and company media to promote the activities and to share esteem. Have some really unique rewards, such as a luncheon hosted by the CEO for the winners of special activities. Utilize nice certificates and letters of commendation signed by the CEO. And always be prepared to go on to the next step.

Above all, have fun with the incentive program. Use the normal desire of people to depart from routine activities to the company's advantage. For just as men and women look forward to bridge tournaments, poker clubs, state fairs, vacations, and holidays, so a departure from the norm can capture the imagination of virtually everyone in a company. Work *with* rather than *against* the grain of human motivation and personality, as you do in all your activities as a manager. Have the typical incentive program last for four weeks, and have Monday morning drawings for prizes for the people who are actually participating by taking the pledge. This will give the entire group something to talk about all week. Make some prizes really worthwhile, of course, and slant everything toward ongoing participation as an achievement community.

Employee Performance Teams

I recently met with some Asian clients, who were quite amused by the American and Australian responses to their competition. They were polite, of course, but they found it very funny that we are just now moving toward quality circles. It was their opinion that we had better jump past such an "outmoded" concept, for throughout Japan, the emphasis is now on performance teams. They implied that our search for a panacea in quality circles is another case of too little and too late for the English-speaking world.

In this final section of the book, I shall look beyond quality circles to *performance teams* in which both quality and productivity are combined for the good of the organization and all its people. Keep in mind the fact that employees cannot be tricked into giving something for nothing; they cannot be persuaded to commit themselves for a panacea.

Performance teams must be the drawing together of everything from a sound philosophy of service— including the utilization of sound interpersonal relationships—to the granting of first-class citizenship to all employees and an equitable sharing of the rewards among the employees.

One of the worst mistakes made by organizations

today is trying to keep the employees' pay as low as possible. This is probably the worst penny-wise-and-pound-foolish decision made by financial men who have no understanding of human psychology as it relates to productivity. I had thought that Henry Ford settled that in 1914 when he raised the pay of his employees from $2.34 a day to $5 per day. All the other managers in Detroit screamed like stuck pigs, but the production genius went right on with his decision like the good Controller he was.

Some years later, Ford said, "The payment of the $5 a day for an eight-hour day was one of the finest cost-cutting moves we ever made, and the $6 a day was cheaper than the $5 day." Unfortunately, managers with no insight into motivation cling to the foolish view that it pays to keep wages to a minimum. All the relevant research shows that it does no such thing.

Of course, the problem of Western civilization will *not* be resolved by granting the workers of our organizations a massive raise. Our leadership failure is too great for that, and part of the failure has been the willingness of managers to buy labor compliance rather than commitment by granting the workers more than they deserved. Ford Motor Company, under Henry Ford's grandson, made this crucial mistake as did the American steel companies, whose wages rose by 221% from 1971 to 1981 while productivity increased only by 15.2%. The rationalization that wage increases could be automatically passed on to the consumers came to a sudden halt when the

Asians and Europeans held to a better proportion of costs and prices.

On the other hand, many companies have shown a dramatic increase in productivity, growth, and profits by granting pay increases that were accompanied by increased employee involvement and productivity. We need leaders experienced in dealing with the employees of the organization in order to regain the productivity needed to become competitive with our adversaries.

There is a small company in Rockford, Illinois— Eclipse Incorporated—that manufactures industrial heaters of various kinds . In 1978, more than 600 of its 650 employees quit and had to be replaced. Most people left because of low wages and the company's determination to produce in spite of untrained, uncommitted employees. Absenteeism was about 10% each day, and earnings had been slipping for five years.

Evidently, the destabilization factor became serious enough for the management group to seek a better way of dealing with their problems. The group chose to win the commitment of the employees in several ways, including participation in decision making and a more equitable sharing of the monetary rewards of commitment. The planning group chose to start with a productivity incentive program that was based both on individual and team performance. Merit interviews were scheduled for all employees from the president to the newest sheet-metal helper. The company moved from confusion to communication to cooperation in one year, and the bottom line reflected it.

Employee turnover dropped from 95% to less than 20% per year. Absenteeism subsided more than 7% but labor costs rose by one-third—enough to make an accountant swear off participation forever. On the other hand, shipping volume rose 65% per employee, and the company profits increased 600%!

Another example is the Muskegon Piston Ring Company, which moved from a million-dollar-a-year loss with its equipment operating at 40% capacity to a million dollar profit the *following year* with its equipment operating at 80% capacity. There are a hundred more examples I could give, all of which would move me to say once again: There are no bad regiments—there are only bad colonels.

Anytime an organization's leaders contemplate change, they can anticipate resistance. Many people have physical and emotional investments in the status quo; in addition, there is the normal inertia of human organizations. Some resistance will come from management and some from the leaders in organized labor. Some people will resist change because they prefer prestige and power to productivity and profits. Others will sincerely doubt that the changes will work well since they have never been tried before in their specific organization. Some people will simply be tired and will resist anything that creates waves for them.

In dealing with organized labor, keep in mind one fact that many managers seem to forget. The only reason that a union has power in any company is because the rank-and-file employees don't trust the managers. In many organizations, the employees feel a need for protection, but if you can nullify that fear of management, you can develop good relationships with your people in a very short while. After all, men and women do not especially enjoy attending long meetings, paying part of their pay to support union activities, and being told to strike because of problems in a distant city.

When the managers of Harmon International and Coors Brewery of Golden, Colorado, built links of trust and mutual support with the employees, great changes occurred. At the Coors Brewery, the people moved to decertify the union because they felt no need for it, although the Harmon employees retained the union there.

When the managers choose to win active employee commitment through the establishment of performance teams that share equitably in company rewards, some ground rules should first be established.

Work with labor leaders while offering better wages that are accompanied by controls, standards, and accountability from each person in the team.

Use the performance team concept to attract better employees, pay them better wages than they can earn anywhere else in the community, and plan for more from them as worker/capitalists.

Give people the opportunity to set their own income and to produce because it is now personally important for them to produce.

Insist on growth from your people, culling out and replacing those who have been too hurt to appreciate the opportunity you offer, as you insist on outstanding quality and quantity.

In your meetings with employees and labor representatives, stress that a new era is beginning, a time of cooperation and trust that shall follow because you are determined to make the necessary adjustments and compromises until others are convinced of your sincerity. Have the facts needed to demonstrate the need for performance teams because of the competition, show how their use will benefit everyone in the company, but expect that people will respond emotionally rather than to facts alone. As you plan for change, use any destabilizing factors that occur, or create them if necessary. Give the union people reasons to change, and then restabilize at a new level of trust and cooperation. However, don't be like one bank manager who wanted to implement a new balancing procedure despite the resistance of his counter employees. When they refused to accept his method, he stopped arguing and, from time to time, quietly dropped a nickle or two into their cash drawers. At night, their drawers didn't balance, of course, and the situation became quite unstable emotionally. Finally, when he suggested the procedure again, the employees were so unhappy that they accepted it at once. I shudder to think what would have happened to their trust had the group discovered his Machiavellian approach to change, however.

Plan the organization of performance teams about a year in advance. It will take that long to move from confusion, through communication, to cooperation. It isn't accidental that my Productivity Improvement System requires a year to complete once the group starts developing a conscious philosophy of service. The organization of well-run performance teams is the climax of the entire program, and it requires about a year to have them organized and working well.

Convince the employees, supervisors, managers, and shareholders that the new approach to teamwork is the most important thing that has happened to the company in years. Convince them that this is, indeed, a new relationship in which each employee contributes as best he or she can and is rewarded accordingly. Begin the actual organization of performance teams, after the groundwork of communication has occurred, by selecting core groups from across the entire company. Bring in craftsmen, secretaries, supervisors, salespeople, managers, engineers, and accountants to help the development team draw together all the crucial factors that relate to improved productivity and quality. Have those people work as in-house consultants.

At one of the planning meetings Harmon International held, a grizzled welding foreman challenged a young architect's choice of equipment for a new facility. He rolled up his pant leg and revealed an ugly scar on his calf. "This," he announced to the group, "is what can happen if we choose that kind of setup." The group shuddered collectively and sent the young man back to his drawing board, sadder but wiser for his encounter with the core group and its specialists.

Train your core group to help the discussion leaders who will be chosen by their peers to conduct the actual meetings of the performance teams. Train the discussion leaders to begin by examining, with their associates, the most serious problem facing the group. The problems can be hardware or software related. Teach them to select a single most serious problem from the list offered by their fellow workers and to spend time during the following week seeking a solution to that problem. When the group meets the following week or fortnight, they will discuss and choose the best solution and report that to the secretary, who will also be chosen from the group. The secretary will write up the results and turn in the statement to the proper evaluation team set up for that purpose. The evaluation team will work with the supervisors, managers, and team leaders to see how the new approach is working and whether it should be used more broadly. One half-day program will be enough to train the performance team leaders immediately after their selection by their peers.

After the most serious problem has been resolved regarding both quality and productivity, the group will then deal with the second most challenging problem and so on in order. At the end of a few months, virtually every problem faced by a work group will have been brought into the open, discussed freely, and acted upon. The results can be outstanding.

As with the use of incentive programs, the CEO of an organization must be supportive of the activity. The CEO should speak at various meetings, reward teams that become outstanding, and generally take part in the continuation of productive activities. To delegate it to an assistant is to notify the entire organization that it is not all that serious, though a deputy should be used to carry out the details most of the time.

Plan ahead to develop a profit from a true partnership with the employees. Form a mutually supportive relationship that harnesses the psychological and spiritual needs which are so often ignored by companies because they are subjective rather than objective. Finally, become like the Viking longship that could consistently outsail a galley three miles to two.

We frequently use the analogy of a ship in a stormy sea to describe our organizations. This is an apt comparison, but the famed longships were faster and better because of one basic factor. They did have better sails and a better hull design, but most of all they had better seamen.

The captain owned the longship, but each Viking came aboard with his own oar. He had carved it laboriously the previous winter, and he joined the crew with a personal involvement. His earnings—his very life itself—depended upon his skills and strength being blended in with the decisions of the captain and the cooperation of the crew. His ideas were considered in the moot where decisions were made;

he was a free man of worth to the entire crew; he had a piece of the action in all that was gained in trading or in raiding. He never had to be chained to the oars!

I'm not recommending that American, Australian, Asian, Canadian, and British businesspeople become pirates. I do insist that they work to create a similar community in which boldness and initiative are rewarded when people work hard together on projects that are important to them personally. To put it another way, when a company gives its people skimpy rewards—be they financial or otherwise—the company receives limited productivity. When it gives average rewards, it receives average productivity. But when an organization breaks out of the adversarial mold to offer its people the chance to win special rewards—and connects the rewards to commitment in a community—the company receives exceptional productivity and astonishing quality.

Conclusion (Only For *Ambitious* Readers)

The changes of our era, discussed in considerable detail in preceding chapters, create massive problems for managers who cling to the past or who work in organizations where the management team relies on an illusion of interpersonal power to reach company goals. Ambitious, perceptive managers must mature beyond illusions, abandon the use of panaceas, and create a community of achievers in which the first-class citizens have consistent, legitimate reasons to dedicate themselves to the organization and its leaders.

The suggestions that follow have proven especially valuable for my Western and Eastern clients:

- Develop and widely promote, for consistent utilization within the organization, a sound philosophy of service that creates first-class citizenship for all members and an equitable sharing of the physical, pschological, and spiritual rewards of participation. Insist that the philosophy of the organization include the areas of management, motivation, and productivity.

- Strive for smallness in relationships rather than largeness. Gather people together into performance teams so men and women can identify with people who are important to themselves personally. Few employees can or will identify with a massive headquarters group in a distant location, but virtually everyone will support, respect, and trust leaders who help them reach personal goals. Cluster men and women together in growth centers from which people find consistent satisfaction because they are doing important things with important people—their friends and peers.

- Develop new ways to draw employees, in large numbers, into the decision-making processes of the organization. When people make important decisions about their work, the decisions then become their own choices rather than something imposed, willy-nilly, from some distant or dominant manager. Select core groups to make recommendations and decisions about facilities, work standards, safety regulations, new products, quotas, contract bids, and everything that is important to the organization's well-being. Harness the fact that collectively the employees know everything that takes place in the company as well as everything that should occur.

- Establish a counseling or an ombudsman program to deal with problems and stresses that sometimes occur when organizations experience rapid change. Give the employee a counselor who cares and who works outside the regular chain of command. Give the ombudsman freedom to deal with problems without being fearful of disturbed managers.

- Put an end to the interminable, open-ended assignments that destroy creativity and commitment. When people have mastered their jobs, move them around even though doing so goes against the conventional wisdom of the Industrial Engineering approach. Remember that we have suffered our massive leadership failure while using the best systems ever designed. Take the time to enable people to grow in skill and in worth.

- Modify or even eliminate the traditional chain of command that evolved in the Prussian army of Frederick the Great and was transplanted to the Connecticut Valley during the Industrial Revolution. It is a lockstep approach that evolved around the use of a water-wheel to power the plan through a complicated belt system. If your organization no longer uses a water-wheel for power, discard the system that evolved with it. Organize with a circular or a cloverleaf method of getting tasks done so the employees deal with one another directly rather than through several tiers of managers who always know less about the work than the people doing it. Refuse to let a fearful or a selfish manager block the flow of crucial information that should be moving freely in all directions in contemporary organizations.

- Teach managers and supervisors to understand and use the principle of motivation—that people are always committed to doing things that have become important to them personally and will never be committed to doing things that are not personally important. Insist that managers work beyond the simple pleasure/pain principle taught by Freud and Skinner, beyond the power/prestige principle taught by Adler and Berne, to utilize the purpose/permanence principle taught by Frankl and DeVille. To be motivated and committed, employees not only need to *have* things of value, they must also *do* things that are important, and *become* what they have the ability to become. This is part of the process of maturing as a person, and there is no reason why business and commercial organizations cannot profit as they help men and women mature in worth.

- Finally, draw together the concepts and methods that create a community of achievers in which people work both hard and smart because they want to—because it is to their perceived benefit to cooperate. End any and all company practices and policies that rely on a bankrupt philosophy of power—of officers and enlisted men, of nobles and peasants. Neutralize or eliminate people in authority who still prefer personal prestige to productivity and profits, or who want things to remain unchanged until they retire. Insist that prestige be earned and shared. Harness everything your people have learned about creativity, commitment, and productivity from the behavioral sciences. Set the stage for people, at every level of responsibility, to achieve because it is in their best interest to do so.

Dana Corporation, Harmon International, E.I. Lilly, Hewlett-Packard, Dayton-Hudson, The Hillside Clinic, John's Brick Yard—these are but a few of the organizations that have done very well by becoming communities of achievers. In these organizations, the managers:

1. *Manage interpersonal relationships very well*
2. *Share the rewards of achievement equitably*
3. *Require first-class citizenship of all employees*

Dana Corporation is a class apart. It employs around 30,000 people in normal times and is high on the Fortune 500 list. *Fortune* editors call it the best-managed corporation in the United States. Certainly, it is one of the fastest growing organizations in the world. It reached that status after Chairman Jerry Mitchell said:

There's no magic in what we do. We set out to create a humanistic climate in which people would benefit from and accept change.

There is magic, however, in Mitchell's brilliance. He began by giving the corporation away—by replacing the 18-inch-thick policy manual with a single sheet that was actually the revitalized company's philosophy of service to the managers of some 90 factories and 400 facilities. Each manager received virtually complete autonomy to make his own capital decisions, to buy materials, to fabricate them as his management team decided, and to sell at the best possible price. Instead of decentralizing into *profit centers*, however, Dana actually became a network of *growth centers!* Then, twice a year, all the managers gather for Hell Week, at which time they must report to Mitchell and the other managers what has been accomplished with the resources and relationships at hand. I have heard it said that it can be a humbling experience for some!

Then there are the rank-and-file employees of Dana. In the industrial world, where 20% turnover is normal, if not a bit low, Dana typically has less than 300 employees leave out of a group of 30,000. Employees own significant amounts of stock that they purchased at market prices, and labor troubles are unheard of. Dana is on a roll because a very bright and tough CEO understood that *he* had to make the changes, not those delegated by him. He took the company by the horns, and created something that should be an example for any manager.

I could tell a similar story about Richard Harmon from Harmon International, but John's Brick Yard should be mentioned at the other extreme. John Parkinson was a graduate student of mine some years ago. He was majoring in psychology when his father died, leaving the family company in the hands of John, the oldest son. Just before returning home to Califor nia, John visited me to ask for suggestions. I advised him to use the concept he had learned. He did, and two years later returned with a success story that rivals Dana's in efficiency, if not size. Parkinson told me:

I went home and spent several weeks looking things over. I investigated the equipment, the market, our customers, and our finances. For- tunately, Dad left things solid, with no large debts and with two good foremen.

After my research was complete, I made my plans and called the entire group together, all 29 of them and the secretary. We took an afternoon off together, had lunch at the beach park, and I spelled out what I believed would be best.

I told them that I had the distinct feeling that Dad had enjoyed piddling around at a brick .yard, and that he hired men that would put no pressure on him. To me, I continued, the yard was a means to an end—and I suspected that it was largely a job to them also. Therefore, I said, I had a proposal for the workers.

I wanted a 50% increase in bricks with no greater investment in equipment or labor. In fact, I insisted on that productivity increase. Professor, it got so quiet that you could have heard the proverbial pin fall into the sand. I mean, they were unhappy with me, so I went on to drop the other shoe, so to speak.

I told the workers that I was perfectly willing to give something in return. For that 50% increase in bricks, I would get rid of the time clocks and put everyone on a salary like the foremen. They would need only to call their foreman if a child needed to go to a dentist or whatever. We would also break into teams to meet regularly to deal with ideas, suggestions, and problems. Then I got down to the nitty-gritty. I told them that I would sell the extra bricks and give them a bonus of half of everything we made the sale.

I would add their bonus money to their bi-weekly paychecks, or invest it until Christmas, put it into an IRA, or place it in some other package for their children's education. There was a lot of grinning at that point, and then I gave them the last shot. I told them that from now on, as soon as we reached our quota each day I would blow the whistle and we would all go home.

John went on to say that the hardest problem to resolve, after selling all those extra bricks, was finding an afternoon golf partner at the club. The only time the group didn't make the quota by mid-afternoon was when two of the kilns broke down on the same day. Otherwise, by 3:00 or 3:30 the men from the crew were relaxing on the front porches of their homes. There was no employee turnover, no malingering, and no adversary relationship. Any time a new employee didn't understand the requirement of participation, a committee from the kiln room met him or her in the parking lot and spelled it out. Shape up or ship out!

Later, when John decided to go into the production of roofing tiles and clay tile pipe, he called another meeting, confessed his ignorance about the change, and asked for suggestions. The group did prove to have total recall about pipe and tile, so he received advice regarding the kinds of equipment and people needed. He followed their suggestions and, when he advertised for six more employees, more than 500 applicants showed up. The workers of the community had learned who was getting the best pay, saving for their kids' education, and sitting on the stoop drinking beer at 3:30 in the afternoon!

If John's Brick Yard continues to expand, he will have to abandon the entrepreneurial approach, but I am convinced that he will integrate professional management practices with the concern he has for people and their commitment to the group. It may be that he will see that the organization never stops working as a community of achievers, even if considerable growth does occur.

Outstanding productivity and excellent quality can be won in our society just as surely as it is achieved in Japan and Europe. Excellence that is obtained because men and women want esteem, participation in important activities, and rewards for working hard, is not limited to any one society or culture. All humans share these needs which can be capitalized on by managers to create communities of achievers.

Good luck in your quest to rise above the pack, to develop a spirit of excellence in your organization, and to grow as an individual and as a member of an outstanding group.

Index

Index

Recommended MENTOR Books

MENTOR and SIGNET Books of Related Interest

Buy them at your local

bookstore or use coupon

on next page for ordering.

Computers Made Simple with SIGNET

(0451)

☐ **PORTER'S PROGRAMS FOR THE IBM PCjr** by Kent Porter.
(820886—$6.95)

☐ **PORTER'S PROGRAMS FOR THE COMMODORE 64** by Kent Porter.
(820908—$6.95)

☐ **PORTER'S PROGRAMS FOR THE APPLE® II FAMILY** by Kent Porter.
(821076—$6.95)

☐ **THE NEW AMERICAN COMPUTER DICTIONARY** by Kent Porter.
(132920—$3.95)

☐ **AN EASY-TO-UNDERSTAND GUIDE TO HOME COMPUTERS** from *Consumer Guide®*.
(120310—$3.95)

☐ **1985 COMPUTER BUYING GUIDE** from *Consumer Guide®*.
(132440—$4.50)

☐ **UNDERSTANDING MICROCOMPUTERS** by R. Deakin.   (124278—$3.50)*

☐ **THE TIMEX PERSONAL COMPUTER MADE SIMPLE** by J. Siminoff.
(121384—$3.50)

*Not available in Canada.
Prices higher in Canada.

Buy them at your local bookstore or use this convenient coupon for ordering.

NEW AMERICAN LIBRARY,
P.O. Box 999, Bergenfield, New Jersey 07621

Please send me the books I have checked above. I am enclosing $_____ (please add $1.00 to this order to cover postage and handling). Send check or money order—no cash or C.O.D.'s. Prices and numbers are subject to change without notice.

Name_____

Address_____

City_____State_____Zip Code_____
Allow 4-6 weeks for delivery.
This offer is subject to withdrawal without notice.